The Journal of *Lady Aberdeen*

THE OKANAGAN VALLEY IN THE NINETIES

1986

Morriss Publishing Ltd.
VICTORIA, BRITISH COLUMBIA

The Journal of *Lady Aberdeen*

THE OKANAGAN VALLEY IN THE NINETIES

Annotated and Edited by
R. M. MIDDLETON

ISBN 0-919203-67-1

FIRST PRINTING NOVEMBER 1986
SECOND PRINTING JULY 1989

Published by
MORRISS PUBLISHING LTD.
1745 Blanshard Street
Victoria, British Columbia
V8W 2J8

Designed and printed in Canada by
MORRISS PRINTING COMPANY LTD.
Victoria, British Columbia

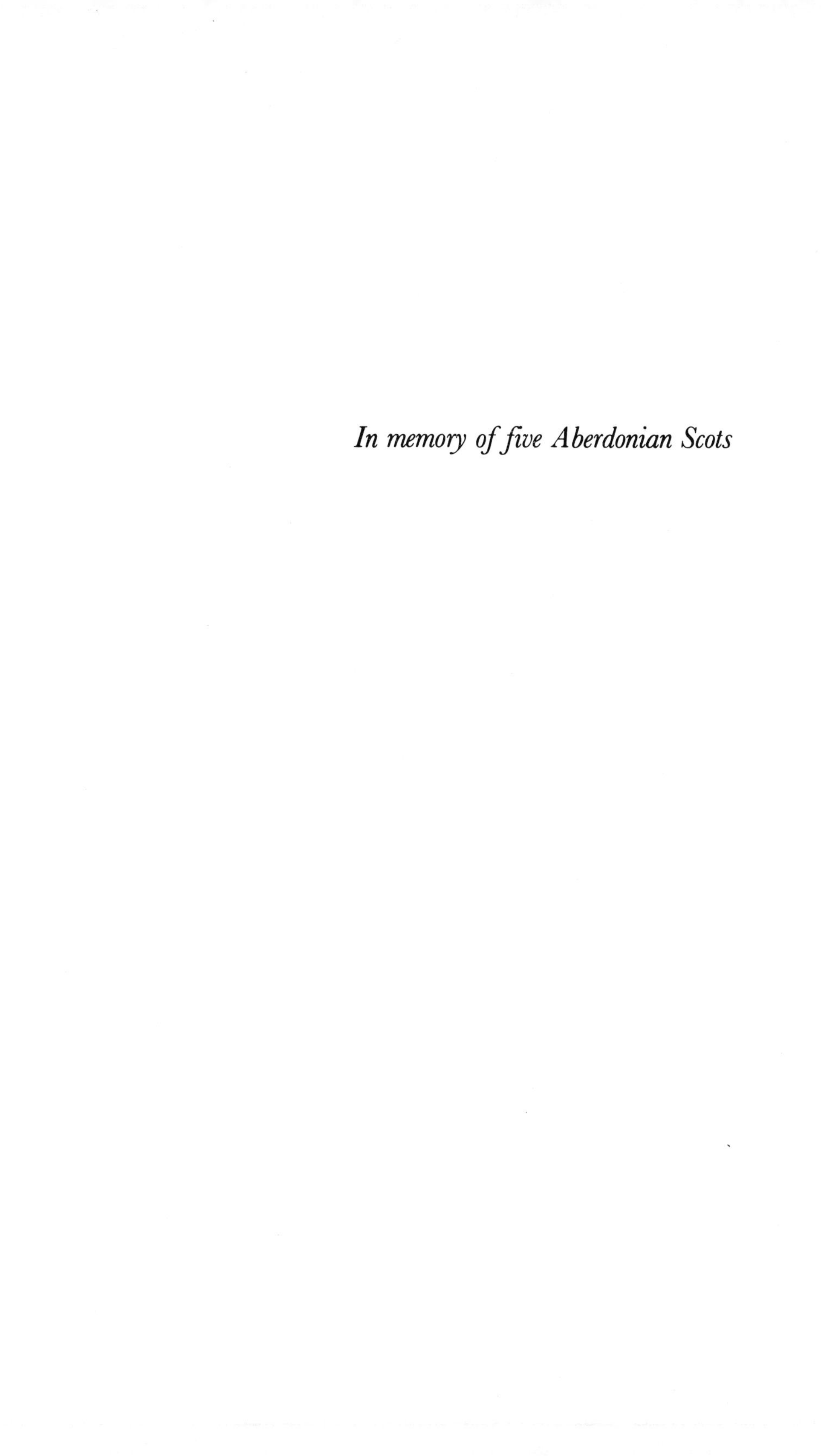

In memory of five Aberdonian Scots

"It is a gloriously beautiful country as to scenery and climate. . . ."

Lady Aberdeen, October 8, 1895

"This year there will be a big deficit in the income as compared with the expenses."

Lady Aberdeen, October 30, 1894

CONTENTS

FOREWORD

BY THE MARQUESS OF ABERDEEN

My family are greatly indebted to Robert Middleton for editing and publishing my grandmother's observations and recollections on the Okanagan Valley in British Columbia. They shed new light on a remarkable woman, described by Lord Hailsham at my father's memorial service as "brilliant and eccentric."

She was decades ahead of her time in doing welfare work amongst rural communities. The gift of patronage (in its best sense) was her legacy to the many organizations, now world-wide, that are devoted to making life more interesting for people who cannot quite manage for themselves.

This journal reveals my grandparents' pioneering spirit and also—sadly—their almost innocent lack of a nose for money. They allowed a fortune to slip through their fingers.

Further comment I will not make for the Journal speaks eloquently for itself.

What I *can* do is write some further illumination through personal knowledge of Granny. She died when I was 19, just old enough to appreciate that, once having known her, no woman —not even Queen Mary—could overawe me.

Granny was a Battle-Axe: I must quickly explain the true nature of this now extinct species. They ruled by sheer force of personality and not by bullying. They never competed with each other in hat-pin to hat-pin confrontation, being much too shrewd to be seen in vulgar competitiveness.

So they stayed each in their own territory; when they did meet they *combined*, which of course made them twice as formidable.

When a lesser but intelligent mortal stood up to them they won respect by listening. To be reasonable and open to constructive argument gave them, paradoxically, even greater dominance.

Such a person, then, was Granny. As a child and as a young man I never attempted any overt act. The limit of my ambition was to please. Any miscalculation or misdemeanour was met by a quiet voice that made one jump a foot in the air. Granny never raised her voice; she did not need to. I was told once by an old Russian princess that she "had seen Lady Aberdeen walk onto a platform and 5,000 people fell silent."

As she got older she became larger and larger, but there was little slackening of mental energy.

Every day between 300 and 400 letters came by special postal delivery. After dinner she retired to her study with her secretary and occasionally my grandfather (neither of whom could keep up with her) and they worked on the correspondence all through the night. At dawn she went up to bed—she loved to see the sunrise—and slept for a few hours.

She must have been the despair of the servants, especially the cook because meals, which were lavish, could take place at any old hour. Lunch could be at 1 o'clock or 3:30, dinner equally erratic, all meals seven courses long.

If the daily letter total was not enough her position as more or less perpetual President of the International Council of Women brought her an annual bag of 5,000 Christmas cards.

Poor dear Granny, she once said to my brother in a rare moment of candour and self-exposure, "I suppose we made many mistakes; but I like to think that we did more good than harm."

That, for me, is a fitting epitaph for a great and honest woman.

ALASTAIR ABERDEEN

Quicks Green
Ashampstead
Berkshire

PREFACE

About twenty years ago I learned that the Public Archives of Canada had in its possession the *Journal* of Lady Aberdeen. Her husband, the Earl of Aberdeen, had been Governor-General of Canada from 1893 to 1898, but his name meant more to me than other governors-general before and since because he and Lady Aberdeen had persuaded my grandparents, William and Catherine Middleton, to leave Scotland and settle in the Okanagan, where the Aberdeens had bought extensive properties. I had grown up hearing about them from my father, W. A. Middleton, who remembered them as a small boy. I, therefore, consulted Lady Aberdeen's *Journal* and found in it extensive references to the Okanagan, its early settlers and some of the problems that they faced. This led me to other autobiographical and biographical material and I put it all together in a rough manuscript, essentially for the interest of my father.

Because primary source material on the Okanagan in the 1890s is limited and because the Aberdeens made such an important contribution to the early development of the Okanagan I decided a few years ago that I should share with a wider readership some of Lady Aberdeen's observations and, without attempting any scholarly analysis, give some insights into the difficulties they encountered. To supplement the writings of the Aberdeen family I also consulted papers in the Scottish National Archives for further details on the very early days of the Guisachan and Coldstream ranches and selected a large number of photographs. Most of them are taken from albums at Haddo House, the seat of the Aberdeen family in Scotland. To the best of my knowledge, they have not been published before. As I was going through them I came across a photograph of my own grandparents and their young family taken over ninety years ago just before they left for Canada. This was a fitting end to my research as that in a sense was the cause of it all.

I would like to thank the present Marquess of Aberdeen for the foreword that he kindly wrote, the National Trust of Scotland and June, Marchioness of Aberdeen for making available to me certain material at Haddo House, and the British Columbia Heritage Trust for their contribution towards the cost of publishing this book. I am also indebted to Professor John Saywell for allowing me to quote lengthy extracts from his book on Lady Aberdeen. Finally, I much appreciated the suggestions given to me by my brother and sister-in-law, Douglas and Evelyn Middleton, which helped me to get this modest work published.

R. M. MIDDLETON

CHAPTER I

The Aberdeens and Canada

John Campbell Gordon, seventh Earl of Aberdeen and first Marquess of Aberdeen and Temair, was born in Edinburgh on August 3, 1847. He studied at St. Andrews University and later at University College, Oxford. He unexpectedly succeeded to the title in 1870 after the accidental deaths in succession of his two elder brothers. A Gladstonian Liberal, he was appointed Lord Lieutenant of Ireland in 1886, but resigned his post a few months later upon the defeat of the government. In 1893, after the return of the Liberals to office, he went to Canada as Governor-General where he remained until 1898. In 1906 he was appointed once more to Dublin as Lord Lieutenant for the unusually long term of nine years. He worked hard and successfully for better relations between London and Dublin, but he was also popular amongst the Irish at large. He retired to Aberdeenshire in 1915 and died in 1934.

Lord Aberdeen married Ishbel Maria Marjoribanks in 1877. She was born in London on March 14, 1857, the youngest daughter of the first Lord Tweedmouth. Theirs was an extremely happy marriage and in their later years they called themselves and were known as "We Twa." Perhaps even more than her husband Lady Aberdeen had a highly developed social conscience. One of their earliest enterprises was the Haddo House Association, an educational and recreational project for the tenants on their estates, which over time extended its membership throughout Britain and the Empire as the Onward and Upward Association. In Ireland Lady Aberdeen launched the Women's National Health Association which devoted itself to maternal and child welfare including a successful crusade against tuberculosis. In Canada she was the first president of the National Council of Women, which sought to improve the political, social and economic position of women. She founded the Victorian Order of Nurses and the May Court Club, a charitable organization. She led a delegation of the International Council of Women to the Versailles Conference in 1919 and, in a farsighted initiative for its day, persuaded the League of Nations to open posts on its Secretariat to women on an equal basis with men. She was one of the first women to be made a justice of the peace and was the recipient of many honours — British, Canadian and foreign. She remained vigorous to the end of her life and died in Aberdeen in 1939.

In the words of Professor Saywell,[1] the Aberdeens "had much in common and their differences although striking were complementary. Aberdeen was a godly man, gentle and humble, self-effacing; Lady Aberdeen was intense and passionate, confident and aggressive, learning only with great difficulty to control the Marjoribanks temper . . . they were both affable and generous, almost to a fault. Both were intelligent, but Lady Aberdeen's mind was the more critical; his the more tolerant and understanding. Their religious backgrounds brought them both to see the true worship of God in the service of man." The Aberdeens devoted much of their energies and fortune to one public cause or another to improve the lot of what today would be called the underprivileged. In the social reforms which they either advocated or assisted to implement, in the organizations which they set up and the way they went about giving help, they were often years ahead of their time.

The Aberdeens visited Canada in 1890, and 1891, but returned in 1893 to stay for five years when, as was mentioned earlier, Lord Aberdeen was appointed Governor-General. The *Journal* kept by Lady Aberdeen of her time in Canada is "the most important single manuscript for the mid 1890s and ranks with the major manuscript collections" in the light it throws on some of the most critical years in the country's history. Lady Aberdeen was not only an acute observer, but more important her political and religious convictions, her personality and experience alike demanded that she be a participant.

She above all was not, could not be, content to be a figurehead, the captive of Canadian society. Almost at once she seized the initiative and retained it for the five years they remained in Canada. Aberdeen often followed where she bravely led.

Lady Aberdeen was thirty-six when she arrived (to live) in Canada. She was a big handsome woman, with a warm soft personality that seemed to reach out and envelop her friends and associates. Inwardly reserved and shy, outwardly she possessed a compelling frankness and an infectious, somewhat boyish, gaiety; secretly often depressed and fearful, she maintained a front of unshakeable optimism. She was that peculiar combination of a democrat-aristocrat. She could work with people of all kinds, ignoring distinctions of birth and occupation, airing views that bordered on socialism, and supporting trade unions and co-operatives. Within the Haddo House Club or the Household Club, as it was known in Ottawa, the Aberdeens fraternized with the staff in working parties and social evenings. Yet in appearance and manner Lady Aberdeen was every inch a grande dame of the aristocracy who could when she chose mount the pedestal of her position and gaze coldly upon those who had presumed upon her democratic spirit. As Katharine Tynan wrote, "the divinity that doth hedge a king was very much to be felt in the case of Lord and Lady Aberdeen, despite their simplicity and friendliness."

Someone once remarked that Lady Aberdeen was an "autocrat-democrat" and that description is also appropriate. She had incredible energy, uncommon powers of organization, and enough experience to give her poise and self-confidence. Whatever the occasion she seemed to dominate it. This not only emerges from the *Journal*, but is also revealed by contemporaries such as Katharine Tynan, who worked with her for many years: "She had no understudy, nobody could take her place. The meetings were dull and dead without her. As soon as she arrived it was like the Palace of the Sleeping Beauty. Everything that had been dead and dusty came alive: the clock had struck, and all was life and energy." She was at times too zealous, too overbearing, too frankly critical. But the work got done.

Lord Aberdeen was delicate in appearance, with smooth dark hair and beard encasing soft sympathetic eyes. His appearance betokened his manner, which was marked by an exquisite courtesy, graciousness, and simplicity. Never vulgar and personally sensitive, he was also deeply aware of the feelings of others. He was a good speaker and an excellent raconteur, and although too high-minded and moralistic for his Canadian audiences, usually managed to find a popular touch. Aberdeen was not tough-minded, however, and even in his official duties as Governor-General often leaned on his wife for support and direction.

Of the two Lord Aberdeen was perhaps more inclined to accept much of life as he found it. While his wife lamented the preoccupation with sports in Canada, because it took people away from more worthwhile pursuits, he entered into them with enthusiasm. He was an expert curler, a proficient skater, and a superb horseman. He enjoyed his apprenticeship on a bicycle and spent an evening with a log-running crew on the Gatineau. He commonly attended hockey and lacrosse games and earnestly entreated the athletes to keep the game clean. In time Lady Aberdeen not only became reconciled to this side of Canadian life, but came to enjoy it.

The Aberdeens also had their personal problems. Sometimes the pace became too feverish and Lady Aberdeen would be driven to bed with the blinding headaches that were the legacy of (an) earlier breakdown. Like all immigrants they were often homesick. As she wrote to a friend not long after their arrival: "... home sickness seems to be an abominable sort of lingering malady that will neither die nor cure; 5 or 6 years away look horribly long." The restraints of an official position as well as the Conservative outlook or confined interests of most of their entourage sometimes weighed heavily on her natural buoyancy, but she consoled herself as she told her correspondent by putting up "a picture of Mr. G. [Mr. Gladstone] in every room." Their expenses in Canada probably were double their salary, with their liberal entertainments, extensive travel, and generous benefactions, while their own income declined steadily in the face of the agricultural depression. Lady Aberdeen carried the burden of worry. As she burst out to a close friend: "It is a comfort that A. can take things lightly, it would be the last straw if he began to worry. But sometimes I fairly sink under the load...."

Lady Aberdeen had two cures for a depression. The first was to escape from the "stifling artificiality" by a trip, a ride—"I am quite ashamed to find how much better a place the world can look during, and after, a ride"—or a retreat into the library—"as for reading, more and more I find that to keep life in proportion, books are an absolute necessity." The second was to work, to plunge into the matters at hand with a frenzied energy and fierce determination.

There was enough work to be done looking after the children and supervising the staff. The eldest boys, Haddo and Dudley, were at Harrow and Cargilfield, but frequently came to Canada with tutors. Marjorie and Archie, aged twelve and eight when they arrived in Canada, were educated at home. No sooner had they reached Quebec than Lady Aberdeen engaged a French tutor for the entire family, although she was fluent and Lord Aberdeen spoke better French than most Governors-General. Canadian dancing too was an art to be mastered, for the Aberdeens had no desire to force people to follow the court. Canadian history and government likewise demanded intensive study. The staff of seventy needed constant supervision, and Lady Aberdeen took a leading part in the Household Club and was responsible for the discussion of contemporary affairs. Unless they were on holidays at Coldstream or their fishing headquarters at New Richmond (N.B.), hardly a day passed without a visitation or meeting.

They also entertained incessantly. There were of course the State Dinners during the Session and other official entertainments. But the Aberdeens did not stop there. Formal dinners or informal luncheons or suppers were held almost daily as Lady Aberdeen sought to bring influential people together behind some grand project. People co-operated despite themselves. On several occasions they attempted to stimulate interest in Canadian history by an historical tableau or a fancy dress historical ball. During the winter the Saturday afternoon skating and tobogganing parties became an Ottawa favourite and Lord Aberdeen went to considerable expense to enlarge the changing and warming rooms.[1]

It was such a couple who came to the Okanagan. They may only have lived there for a total of four months over half a dozen visits, but because of the position that they held they put the valley on the map not only in Canada but in England and Scotland as well. Their imaginative ideas on the economic and social development of the Okanagan and their willingness to back them up with their own money was a marvellous shot in the arm for the young communities so newly established in the heartland of an immense province.

The principal players in the piece that follows are relatively few, but the initials "A" or, after he became Governor-General, "H. E." are used by Lady Aberdeen and others to refer to her husband while Coutts Marjoribanks is her brother who helped to manage the Guisachan and Coldstream ranches at one time or another. The children of the Aberdeens were Marjorie (later Lady Pentland), George (Lord Haddo), Dudley and Archibald or Archie.

Notes

CHAPTER I

[1] Saywell, J. T., *Canadian Journal of Lady Aberdeen*, Champlain Society, Toronto, 1960, p. xvi, et seq.

CHAPTER II

The Aberdeens and Kelowna

In 1889 Lady Aberdeen suffered a nervous breakdown and her doctors advised a long holiday. She and Lord Aberdeen selected Canada as a place to visit partly because they were interested in emigration as a solution for Britain's social problems. They arrived in August 1890 and after first staying in Hamilton, Ontario, they went by train to Western Canada. They were not impressed by the bleakness of the prairies, but they were so enthralled by what they saw in British Columbia that they wanted to buy some land. It would be for their own enjoyment, but also a means of enticing Coutts Marjoribanks, Lady Aberdeen's brother, to leave North Dakota. He had been living in isolated circumstances on a farm which was not a financial success. They turned to Mr. G. G. Mackay, who had once worked for Lady Aberdeen's father, to help them find a farm. Since they thought that land in the Fraser Valley was too expensive at $50 to $60 an acre, they were attracted, as Lady Aberdeen noted in her *Journal* on October 14, 1890, by Mr. Mackay's suggestion

> ... of another district about 21 hours from Vancouver whose reputation is even better and which is now in the process of being opened up by a railway going south of the CPR to Long Lake which Lord Lorne describes as the loveliest lake in Canada. The railway goes or will go next September to Vernon on the lake. Thirty miles down Okanagan Lake by steamer there is a farm (of) 480 acres with a nice house, some 70 head of cattle, horses, wheat, implements, etc. which Mr. Mackay was thinking of buying on his own account for $10,000 a short time back. The man has some sons who will not help with the work and he cannot do it single-handed.

Mr. Mackay says that he is confident of the value of the land and that in a few years it would sell for double if not four times its present value and he has proved himself so safe and wise a man that we are safe in his hands. The end of it is that A has commissioned Mr. Mackay to buy this place or one like it on his behalf. Then we propose putting Coutts there as manager. Let him be there without salary for two years—then the salary he would have had at £300 a year he will have put £600 into the farm and then he will become partners with A and they will divide the profits... The place besides being on a lake is on a plateau surrounded by hills where the most splendid sport can be had. There is common ground for cattle to graze on and they can winter out. Wheat and fruits and hops will grow and the climate is dryer than on the coast: they have about six weeks of sharp winter in January and February. But I will spare you further details at present as you will doubtless hear enough about it in the future.

Lady Aberdeen's glowing report home of their new property and its potential worth was not well received by her father who, observed somewhat drily that "my calculations will not allow me to think that its size will admit of the capacities you mention. As for the good times you speak of, if they came your way you would be the first people to lay down a double line of railway at your own expense. Well, as usual you are head over ears in business of your own manufacturing."[1]

Despite her father's lack of enthusiasm for it the Aberdeens named the ranch "Guisachan" after one of his estates in Invernessshire. To make it live up to its Gaelic name—"The Place of the Fir"—they planted Scottish fir seedlings. Unfortunately the seedlings died later that year.

The Aberdeens returned home, but after a visit to the United States in the summer of 1891 they went in October to the Guisachan for their first view of their property. They travelled on the first passenger train between Sicamous and Vernon. Lady Aberdeen's description of it is interesting:

Sicamous, October 13th, 1891

Slept in the car last night and taken up by the West-bound train about 7. It was a beautiful day for the magnificent scenery through which we passed—we were much better off than the inhabitants of the prairies where the train encountered a blizzard yesterday. We had several nice halts today (at Field, Donald and Glacier House). ... We arrived here soon after 7—dined in the car, then Marjorie and I repaired to the hotel for the night, A and Turner remaining in possession of the car. We were surprized to find so good an hotel at so small a place but I suppose they are looking to the future, for it is well situated on the Shuswap Lake, noted for its good fishing, lake trout being caught often as big as 15 lb. weight, and then it is the junction for this new Shuswap & Vernon railway, leading down to our country. We saw the Indians spearing fish with a light on the water tonight.

Guisachan, Okanagan Mission, Vernon, B.C. October 14th, 1891

Here we are at last at our destination! The starting of the first passenger train to Vernon was quite an excitement at Sicamous this morning. We were to have come up last night and A had hired a special engine, at the rate of $75 from Mr. Patterson who is in charge of the line until such time as the C.P.R. take it over to work. When we arrived last night at Sicamous, however, Mr. Riley, Mr. Patterson's assistant, told us that Mr. Abbott (the C.P.R. superintendent for the Pacific Division) had asked that the train might be held over till this morning so as to take some people from Vancouver. A was rather disposed to be indignant at first at having his 'special' tampered with but there was consolation to be derived in the fact that we had only to pay half the expenses—at least A suggested that he might be excused half and his suggestion was accepted. The train consisted of the engine, our car, two luggage trucks covered with a miscellaneous assemblage of men, dogs, packages, trunks, agricultural machinery and so forth, and a 'caboose', which I think I am right in describing subject to A's correction, as a sort of glorified guard's van. We were a motley crew and we all got out at the halting places to survey ourselves with mingled pride, interest and curiosity. At one of these places where we stopped to water the engine by means of a primitive contrivance we found quite an orchard and nursery garden right alongside of the track. A went to find out the owner. He (Mr. Thomson) was in at the Vernon First Agricultural Fair, whither we were hurrying for the opening, but he found his son, an intelligent youth, who came into the car and gave us a great deal of information and afterward we met both his father and sister at the Show. They have about 75 acres and are making quite a good thing out of it—cows, and hens, too, which last pays them well at 50 cents per dozen eggs and 50¢ for spring chicken. No cost either for transport, for the Chinamen come round and gather them and sell them. A great part of the journey lay through very pretty country, extremely pretty after leaving Sicamous, skirting the edge of Mara Lake and then through some real big wood, and happily only a little of it burnt; then we came to Enderby, half-way between Sicamous and Vernon where there is quite a little town springing up on the Spallumcheen—as far as this a steamer can come, but from this point we were quite on a new track and we bumped and swerved along in a most marvellous fashion and at times had to creep along at foot's pace—it is indeed only just possible for a train to pass over and large gangs of men are working it still. As we came near Vernon we passed some very settled country and coming as we did, determined not to expect too much, we began to think that things looked very well.

If the Aberdeens had arrived a few days earlier they might have had to travel along the tracks by handcar. Lady Aberdeen admitted that she did not share her husband's enthusiasm for them as a means of transportation. They may have been "cheery little vehicles," but she preferred to walk rather than to "whiz through the air" on them "at the rate of 20 miles an hour."[2]

But to return to Lady Aberdeen's account of the first agricultural fair in Vernon which they stopped to open on their way to the Guisachan:

It was curious that we should almost accidentally hit off the right day when it was first possible to run a passenger train, and also the day for the first Agricultural Exhibition in the district. We should indeed not have known of the Exhibition at all, had it not been for a letter received from my Mother at Banff, telling us what Coutts had told her about it. We had not heard from them direct and we found communication with them very difficult. We must have missed some of their letters and they were generally hazy about the time of our arrival in spite of various efforts to telegraph them. It seems that there is but a telephone from Sicamous to Vernon, and when a message is telephoned, if there happens to be nobody in the office, well there it is, it must take its chance.

So between one mischance and another poor old Coutts had been waiting for us for a whole week at Vernon, and in the crowded state of the primitive hotels there, the wait cannot have been very agreeable. You would scarcely believe, though, that in a place like that, there would be four hotels, and a fifth large one going up under a syndicate, of which Mr. G. G. Mackay is one. It is a little place which evidently means to do—it is the county town—and houses are going up quickly. It is called after the Hon. Mr. Vernon, the Minister for Lands and Works, who has a good deal of property nearby: he was to have opened the Show but was detained at Victoria. So A had been asked (in one of the letters he never got) by the President, Mr. Lumby, to act in his stead and we went around the well known programme of inspecting the show first privately and then publicly and then the regular introduction and speech and vote of thanks. But it was all very nicely done and A spoke excellently. Not too much 'taffy' and all to the point and not too long. The Show in itself was interesting for there were some really magnificent fruits and vegetables shown—monster cabbages and melons and pumpkins and splendid apples. The exhibits from here did well, as we gain six first prizes and six seconds from various articles, pumpkins, garden lemons (funny sort of fruits about the size of peaches growing in the ground and having a sort of acid taste) cucumbers, apples, flowers, etc. Then we went down to the place where the horses and cattle were being shown at the other end of the town and there A bought a team, a pair of mares and a foal for $135—the team promptly took a first prize immediately afterwards and one of the mares with her foal got another first in another class. It was funny to see everything going on just like at home at one of the Shows—the ring and the judges and the animals being led about and the groups of people discussing things in general.

They met several early settlers:

We were introduced to a number of people at the Show. Mr. Dewdney, brother to the ex-Governor and present minister, Hon. E. Dewdney, Government agent at Vernon with Mrs. Dewdney, his second wife, a nice little woman fresh out from England who had made some pretty vases out of tobacco jars and drain(?) pipes and the like for the show—then Mr. Ellison, who got the first prize for apples and gave us some—Mr. Girouard, an old Frenchman, the pioneer settler in these parts in 1858 when it took him the best part of a year to get here from San Francisco, Mr. Tronson, Mr. Lamyn(?) who had an Irish mother and Irish wife and who was interested in Irish Industries; Mr. Stewart, an enterprising young man who has only come this year, but who has started a Vernon

> newspaper and made it pay; Mr. Vernon, a nephew of Mr. Vernon's—The great Mr. Mackay was there too in full force with wife and daughter, just returned from watching over his newly acquired property at Okanagan and as keen and as enthusiastic as ever.

After the fair the Aberdeens proceeded by moonlight down Okanagan Lake in a small boat:

> There we lingered on some time, and so the little steamer boat which was to take us down the lake specially and for which we were supposed to have to wait was ready long before us. The big steamboat 'the Penticton', commanded by Capt. Short and owned by Mr. Ellis of Penticton at the foot of the lake, could not take us as the men had all been given a holiday for the fair and an ensuing ball. The brother of the owner of the small boat, Mr. Leo Lequime, took us down himself and it was a most lovely moonlight night for the four hour trip down the lake. The boat was not properly arranged for passengers and we all sat in a queer little sort of cabin beguiling the time as best we could, A even going the length of improvising a song on the Grand Trunk and the C.P.R. which he and Marjorie sang to the tune of the 'Keel Row'....

They arrived unannounced at Okanagan Mission, and had to walk a couple of miles to the Guisachan. At first they did not get a very warm welcome, but what they saw the next day very much exceeded their expectations:

> At last we turned a little corner and found ourselves in a bay & the landing stage for the Mission near at hand. Owing to the misunderstanding about our arrival, we were not expected, of course; so our friend of the boat (who by the way was going back full speed for the dance at Vernon which would probably go on till 9 next morning) undertook to get a wagon to convey Barron(?) and Turner and some of our baggage, whilst we all walked on the two miles to Guisachan and took possession of our new domain by moonlight. You know Mr. Eustace Smith's letters have not been enthusiastic as to the scenery or anything else and partly because of that and partly because we are getting accustomed to being rather disappointed with places which are so much praised, we were prepared to see just a flat plain with bare hills in the distance, and a few trees and bushes and a house set down in the middle of the flat. Instead of which we found ourselves in the midst of hills looking more like

> Guisachan (Scotland) than any others that we have seen in Canada. About a mile from the landing stage Coutts said 'this is our gate' and we turned in through a regular lodge-like gate into a real wood with big trees of two hundred feet high in it. Right through this wood they have made a new road for us and when you come through at the other side you see the house about a ¼ mile away with a background of very pretty hills. From the house you have a pretty peek of the lake where they have cut away some of the trees for this purpose. The new house seemed very much deserted and locked up when we boarded the verandah, but Coutts knocked away in confidence that someone would appear. Presently a cautious step was heard and Mr. Smith, whom we did not recognize at first with his beard, opened the door a chink and asked what we wanted. It was a pity that we did not keep the fun up and storm the citadel, for he admitted afterwards that he was very suspicious of us and that he had brought his rifle just behind the door to be ready to keep us off.... We could not have had a nicer arrival and our moonlight walk was a much nicer introduction than everything all in readiness. The Chinese cook 'Foo' was soon stirred up and while he prepared something to appease our hunger we had leisure to admire the beauties of the house and the skill with which our two bachelor house-keepers had decorated it. The hall is specially pretty with a sort of gold Japanese paper and arranged with stag horns found lying here, some of Coutts own horns and stuffed heads from Dakota. Then there is a large sitting-room and dining-room, four good bedrooms, two small ones, an office and the kitchen just across a verandah and a verandah running right round the house. It is just perfect and everything is delightful.

This was the fourth house to be built at the Guisachan; the three other previous dwellings still remained standing. The first was the "veriest shack" in which a man could possibly live, the second a small log cabin and the third "quite a substantial house." It had two good living rooms and was currently used by the farm staff. Its ceilings and walls were, however, well riddled with pistol shots which supported the rumours that they had heard of the "wild doings of the younger members of the MacDougal family."[3]

The day after their arrival they went out bear-hunting:

> *October 15th, 1891, Guisachan*
>
> Daylight dispelled none of the fascinations of the place. The

colouring of the hills is warm and their shapes varied and picturesque. Many of them are covered with pine woods and there, mixed with the autumn yellows of the cottonwood and poplar, give much the same effect as our fir and birch, only of course some of the poplar trees are quite big. It was a quiet grayish morning with clear light and misty clouds floating about in the mountains. Gradually it brightened up into sunshine and a lovely sunset. This morning a message came to ask if we would like to go to a bear-hunt, as there was one close at hand.... After luncheon we drove a couple of miles to a neighbour's place called Nicholson's.... We walked up to the scrub where the bear was suffered to be hidden.... But the bush was very thick and prickly and the dogs could scarcely be induced to enter in spite of evident traces of the bear being seen or rather of three—an old one and her two cubs. At last there was moving and shuffling & the sportsmen were intent in their watch when lo and behold Mrs. Bear was to be seen a quarter of a mile away sloping up the hill to the retreat of the fir woods and the two young ones were even wiser for they refused to budge. So we went home without a bag though all three gentlemen discharged all the contents of their rifles at some wild geese which came past us in great flocks filling the air with the whirr of their wings and their peculiar cry. We came upon a lot of prairie chicken too on our road and some wild duck, so had a fair sample of the sport to be had in one afternoon. Neither Coutts nor Mr. Smith had been to a bear-hunt before, partly because they have been so busy watching the house and its builders, and partly because the bears are only now beginning to come down. There has been a scarcity of wild berries this year, which is bringing down more than usual. About a dozen have been killed in the neighbourhood already this season.

October 16, 1891

A magnificent day. Sketched and idled and wandered about. Inspected the old barn and decided there must be a new one, looked at the horses here in addition to the two teams expected back from the Show to-day.... Then we sent Marj off with the two gentlemen to hunt for the pot and A and I pottered about and surveyed everything—the garden still showing splendid cabbages and remains of melons, citrons, cucumbers and one beautiful tree full of apples....

Lady Aberdeen recalled this day again many years later. She remembered that there were plenty of wild geese and wild duck "in several varieties" on Okanagan Lake. There were also "ruffled grouse" which tasted very much like pheasant and prairie chicken which despite its name was in reality a species of pin-tailed grouse, "the best game bird for the table which Canada possesses." They ate bear on one occasion and thought it a good substitute for venison.[4]

The ranch was purchased with livestock "of a mixed character." The cows were so reluctant to earn their keep that they had to be pursued by the cowboys, lassoed, and thrown on their sides before they could be milked. Lady Aberdeen thought all of this was worth the trouble, but admitted that their neighbours bought condensed milk—an interesting comment on the early availability of this item. The rest of the farm animals consisted of some Berkshire pigs, Leghorn chickens and, of course innumerable horses, some of whom were remembered by name in later years. They included the new team bought from Vernon one of which had a foal at foot which "after the fashion of the country" followed along when the horses were hitched up. The team looked smart in their new harness when they were used for the drive to church.

Church loomed large in the mind of Lady Aberdeen. In her *Journal* she commented on the religious life of the young community and mentioned a visit to the Roman Catholic priests at the Mission:

> *October 16th (sic), 1891*
>
> Mr. Langell, the Presbyterian minister, called in the morning. He comes out to this valley from Vernon every Sunday, taking service one week at this end in the schoolhouse and the other at Mr. Postill's at the upper end going back to Vernon (35 miles) for an evening service. A church is now meditated or rather two—a small one at Postill's and a larger one here, for which Mr. Mackay has offered two acres of land near by. Service used to be held at the house of a farmer and a (?) near by, Mr. Brant's, but he wanted the new church up his way and when he heard of Mr. Mackay's offer being accepted, he begged that the service might no more be held at his house. The Trustees of the School, though some of them R.C., gladly gave the school at once. A has promised $400 of the $1,000 required for the new church. Mr. L. seems a straightforward sort of young man originally a Nova Scotian. He has a wife and two

children. Of course, he came with the usual petition that A should take the service to-morrow. This was however declined, as we had already arranged to hold a sort of informal service here in the afternoon when we understood that this was not the Sunday for service here.

In the afternoon Coutts drove us down to the Mission—we called on the priests, Father Marzial, and Father De Vriendt, who are but newcomers, the later priest having only recently left (sic). The Mission was instituted 32 years ago for Indians, but these have now moved away to their reserve at the foot of the lake, so that it is now simply the headquarters of a large district extending to Enderby and the residence of a lay brotherhood, who cultivate a farm, orchard, etc.

She described both the morning church service at the local school and the second service at the Guisachan in the afternoon. While not intended as such the latter turned out to have an agreeable ecumenical flavour:

October 17, 1891

The new pair of substantial mares were hitched to with their new smart harness and all and A drove us after Guisachan fashion to the schoolhouse, the little foal Madge, coming along too, but instead of following, preceding her mother. The scene at the schoolhouse door was one of the prettiest I have seen for a long time. The schoolhouse is situated just at the corner of a wood of tall trees gay in their brilliant autumn colours. Just inside this wood and on its outskirts were tied up saddle-horses and buggies of all sizes and descriptions and all around were standing picturesque groups of men and dogs awaiting the moment for going in. The brilliant sunshine pouring down on us and glinting on the stems of the trees completed the charm and brightness and naturalness of the picture. No conventionality, no black coats (except A's and Mr. Smith's) no solemn looks. There were but three women in the congregation, all the rest men who looked as if they knew how to work. The minister, Mr. Langell, quite adopted the same free and easy attitude and did not talk like a minister. At the end, he announced the service which was to take place in the afternoon at Guisachan and called upon A to give his own invitation. A explained it was meant to be as a sort of exchange of greetings amongst new neighbours in the best way and the congregation dispersed to their several horses and vehicles outside. Fancy the stampede there would be if we tied up all our horses at home anyhow amongst the trees, left them to themselves during service. On our way out, we were introduced to the big people of the Northern end of the valley, the Postills. Mother and son were at the service. She's a dear old Yorkshire lady who prides herself on being the same age as the Queen and is full of kindliness and quiet humour. She was an enchanting figure in her old black stain poke bonnet which she must surely have inherited from her grandmother and with her reminiscences of her arrival in the valley 17 years ago and being the first white woman and the kindness she received from the miners and others. I was so cross at not having my Kodak with me both to photograph her and that scene outside the church door.

After church A and I had a nice wander through our tall wood and then in the afternoon the whole neighbourhood mustered in force for our afternoon service. We were rather taken aback at seeing our two friends the priests appear. A tried to find out if they understood what was up, talked about the chapel at home and so forth; they seemed puzzled but said they came only as listeners and they stayed on right through. We had over 60 people present. A spoke on "Let your light shine before men" and did very well—also told them a little about the Magic Lantern Mission at the end and proposed its being tried here. This was very favourably received and it will be carried out as soon as we can send up a Lantern. Mrs. Postill and her son, the priests, Mr. Rose, Mr. Anderson, a Provincial Govt. Agent at Victoria stopped to tea and we gradually discovered that the priests and some of their flock who had attended had come expecting a political address. Why and wherefore or what politics A was expected to expound, goodness only knows, for the notice put up at the store was simply to the effect that "a short service will be held, etc." However, they did not seem to mind and Father Marzial indeed told A that there was nothing which he could not have said himself.

Lady Aberdeen considered that regular church services were an important ingredient in pioneer life. She had noticed during their trip across Canada that the Presbyterian Church made certain that their adherents were well looked after. Services were held every second Sunday even in quite small communities. Places like Kelowna and Vernon obviously enjoyed services every Sunday. The ministers were provided by the Home Mission Fund until such time as a young community could afford to pay for their own church and minister. The Presbyterians thought it important to give this financial help because they reckoned that left to their own devices settlers might not give proper priority to seeking and paying for ministers themselves and that they would soon get out of the habit of attending church. If this happened Lady Aberdeen believed that "many opportunities for promoting religious influences and for preventing evil will have been lost."[5]

A good Presbyterian, Lady Aberdeen took a poor view of drink in excess and the source for it that was available near the Guisachan. It had a limited relationship to the real estate market, she regretted to note. A good Scotswoman, she also had a healthy awareness of land prices and estimated (somewhat over optimistically as she later learned) the returns on an orchard in the Okanagan:

October 17, 1891

Near by is the "hotel" and store kept by the magnate Lequime—a centre of mischief unhappily to the neighbourhood. It is the custom to repair to this store every Sunday after church and then to sit and drink all afternoon, evening and night, making a frightful row and disturbance. Men often spend all the week's wages there and five small ranches have passed into Lequime's hands in order pay drink accounts—one of those being that part of old Macdougal's land which now lies between us and the lake which we sigh for. Lequime, however, says that anybody who wants it must take the whole of his 8,000 acre ranch along with it at his price 150,000 dollars or leave it. These holders of big pieces of land are greatly impeding the progress of settlement here and are not cultivating their land to any extent themselves. Mr. Mackay however is doing his best by buying several different ranches near here for about 26,000 dollars and by now dividing these up into fruit lots of 40, 60 acres or more. Some of the local people have bought some and now some outsiders are coming in—amongst others a young Mr. Rose, a lad of 18 who comes from near Inverness and has taken a high degree at Aberdeen. He came out here to go in for the law, but finding that profession, like all others, overstocked, he very sensibly has taken to fruit farming. But it seems rather a wretched business for a boy of his age to be here all alone. He is at present lodging with one of our neighbours, Mr. Monson, who has got 60 acres from

> Mackay and is managing the rest of the latter's property besides. We went to call on them this afternoon and found the wife very busy tidying up after being at the Fair at Vernon all the week. It is quite a small house they have, yet besides their own four little boys, they manage to lodge Mr. Rose, Mr. Mackay, Mr. Langell and a good many more besides as she told me she had 14 lodgers this summer to provide for besides the men and children. I cannot say it looks comfy. But to show what even a small orchard will do, take theirs as an example. They have one-third of an acre planted with twenty-four apple trees, some old, some only 4 years old. Last year, after his children, men etc. having lived off apples till the men complained and all picking as many as they chose, he sold 250 dollars worth at 4¢ per lb. So please now calculate what 200 acres planted with apple trees would bring in according to this. Or calculate that they will only bring in half that amount and then say if our farm is not going to pay, even with apples alone. Not that we mean to satisfy ourselves only with apples. Pears, plums, cherries, and then all the small fruits which will bear the second year and so save much waiting. There is an unlimited demand for fruit in the North West, but we are not going to risk the dangers of travelling for the small fruit.

Lady Aberdeen mentioned for the first time their ideas about a jam factory and how its produce would threaten that of Crosse and Blackwell's:

> A is going to put up a jam factory, much to the delight of all the people about, for this is just what was wanted.
>
> Now please rack your heads for good names and advertisements where with to compete with "Crosse and Blackwell" and their likes—"The Premier Preserves manufactured from the celebrated Okanagan Orchards" is the brightest we could think of. Is there nothing that would go with "British Columbia." It would be nice to see poor old Coutts a rich man after all!

Lady Aberdeen, in short, saw enormous promise for the fruit industry in the Okanagan. Two years after her first visit to the Okanagan she wrote in *Through Canada with a Kodak* that she was confident that what she had learned during her stay at the Guisachan meant that the valley would become one of the great fruit producing centres. To make its contribution to this end she would plant two hundred acres of the Guisachan in various kinds of small fruit such as strawberries, raspberries and blackberries. She was convinced that they as well as apples, pears, plums would flourish. Expanding on her *Journal* entry of October 16 just mentioned she said in her book that good land for fruit growing was selling for $30 to $60 an acre. A local landowner with 4,000 to 5,000 acres of range land and 500 acres under cultivation turned down $36,000 for his property and said that he would not take less than $90,000. Good land was worth $60 an acre, he believed.[6]

For some the Okanagan in its early days had its shortcomings on first inspection:

> *October 17, 1891*
>
> Coutts and Mr. Smith are to try to have some sort of Sunday prayers for our own men and anybody else who may care to come. Curiously enough, Coutts seemed to assent more heartily to the proposal than Mr. Eustace Smith. The latter is quite keen now about the fruit culture and is, I think, beginning to settle down, but he took a curious prejudice against the country at first and told several people that he was sure we would be much disappointed. I do not quite understand what he expected—something like East Lothian, I fancy, with made roads and cultivated farms and, above all, he expected a number of young men and others who would form some sort of society. He can surely never have read anything about a new country. It is a pity for it puts him out of sympathy with the people and makes him apt to see the dark side of everything, but I think he will come around in time. Meanwhile he is very valuable in keeping things straight, accounts and letters which Coutts could never manage and he and C seem to get on very well. I rather agree with Mr. Mackay that "if a man cannot be happy here, he cannot be happy anywhere."
>
> An unfortunate incident happened on his way here—not only had he a long way to come by road, but one evening as he was coming along with our foreman, Frank Conkling (a first-rate man) and a waggon load of agricultural machinery, and both were ill, especially Frank, they came to a farm and Mr. Smith asked for a night's lodging. The proprietor absolutely refused to take them in or to let them go into the barn and this gave, very naturally a black idea of Canadian hospitality. But people who know Canada, say that you might have travelled through the length and breadth of Canada without meeting an instance of the sort. In some parts where houses

become regular sort of half-way houses, there is a custom of making travellers pay for their lodging, but there seems no great harm in this. It is unfortunate that this should have happened. [In a footnote, Lady Aberdeen added] It seems that people had made a practice of halting at (this) house and thus saving the cost of going to a Vernon hotel 7 miles further, and apparently this man wanted to let it be known that they would get a cold reception. If so, he certainly succeeded.

In summing up her stay, Lady Aberdeen said how delightful it had been, jokingly added that they would be happy to retire to the Guisachan "when the Revolution at home comes off," spoke of the need for irrigation, described a picnic on Long Lake "the most lovely lake in Canada" and mentioned the installation at the Postills of what must have been one of the earliest telephones in the Valley.

October 23rd 1891, Guisachan

The week has fled away and tomorrow we must say good-bye to this delightful place, where we have enjoyed a more real holiday that we have ever had before. We have sat in the verandah and basked in the sun and read and sketched. We have wandered about settling roads to be made and trees to be cut down, a barn to be built, the site of the jam factory and so forth . . . We have all found it, too, a remarkably healthy place. I have never had the vestige of a headache and we have all been furiously hungry. The only drawback of which we can hear is that the mosquitoes and flies are particularly vigorous during June and July and part of August so avoid these months. We have been fortunate in our weather, but then they rarely have rain—too rarely for purposes of cultivation. Irrigation has therefore to be resorted to and this is now being carried out here, so that we may be independent of rain. What have I more to chronicle? For I must not weary you with our enthusiasm about our new home, to which we meditate retiring when the Revolution at home comes off and which A says he will enjoy possessing much more than he ever did H. H. (Haddo Hall) (well, so far as regards the rented land part, certainly). On Tuesday we made an expedition to Long Lake, which lies alongside of Okanagan on the other side of the hills and which Lord Lorne called "the most lovely lake in Canada." We drove through miles of fir woods which are used as ranges for the cattle. There have been too many cattle on most of this ground and the bunch grass is all eaten down so that the ground looks very sandy, and the grass

> which succeeds this and which is called the "wormwood" has not yet come up. The fir trees are delightful with their red stems and healthy branches and the young trees growing up look very healthy too. We lunched in the wood overlooking Long Lake, decided that though it is very pretty that it does not come up to Okanagan because its shores are barer. Then we drove back to Postill's Lake and took tea there en famille, mother, son and his wife and baby boy and Mr and Mrs Langell and their children. The old lady was much pleased with a telephone just put up communicating between her and her other son 4 miles away. They gave us home-cured ham, home-made jam, home-made bread and then we started for home in the dark by an unknown road, A driving, for Coutts is short-sighted. It soon became very dark and at places Coutts had to walk ahead with a lantern. But we did the 10 miles in 2 hours, which was good going after all under the circumstances and we were rather insulted when Frank came riding out as far as Mr Brant's to meet us and we found that Mr Smith had gone the other way.

The Aberdeens organized at the Guisachan the "first social" ever held in the valley with the guests performing with various degrees of success for one another:

> The other event of the week was the first "social" ever held in the valley, which we got up on Thursday night and which was largely attended in spite of its being a dark night. Father De Vriendt gave two songs, Mr Langell two recitations, Mr Postill three songs to the accompaniment of an American organ lent by Mr Brant. We expected Miss Brant to play but she could not do anything beyond a Sankey's hymn—and Leo Brant and his violin failed us—so the rest of the entertainment consisted in A's speech, two songs and a reading from Nicholas Nickleby, three French songs by Marjorie which brought down the house and two readings of mine. It was quite a success with a tea of course in the middle handed around.

Lady Aberdeen commented on the staff at the Guisachan including the temperament of the Chinese cook:

> The two Chinese cooks did very well on this occasion and indeed our cook Foo does excellently and makes specially good bread and pastry. He is not however so clean as the other whom they have got for the men at the old house and is subject to fits of touchiness which are apt to affect Chinese cooks. For instance, one day a flight of prairie chickens came over the house. A went to get his gun but

meanwhile Foo was seen to go to Coutts' room, grab his gun and cartridges and set forth for the field of action. A told Turner to tell him to wait a bit till he was ready to go, too, and this desperately offended him. He got 3 birds, but nevertheless sulked all day and gave it hot to Turner and Barron. These two latter functionaries have done excellently since we have been here, Barron as housemaid and Turner as man of all work, but I think Barron has entered into it the most of the two. Foo is going to be sent off presently, as the men are leaving during the winter, only Frank Conkling being left and he coming into this house, only one cook will be needed. They seem to have had a nice set of men. One evening we were told that the father of one of our men wanted to see A. A said 'Show him into the office.' But presently, lo and behold, we found that he was a gentleman from Blackheath just arrived from England to see his son. The son has a farm near Calgary, but is working like this to get some money—not an uncommon thing to do—but it is a good illustration of how everybody is mixed up here. Frank Conkling, the foreman, is a working man, shrewd and handy and very hardworking. Coutts knew him in Dakota and brought him along here. He is very valuable and knows something of fruit planting, too. A is going to sell him 10 acres or so at half price and he will bring his father here to make a home. The father knows about fruit, too. Frank gets 50 dollars a month, the others 35 (presumably 25), but they hope it may be 30 next year. This with board, so they are not badly off. Several Aberdeenshire men about here—amongst others, Duncan, foreman of our neighbour Knox's ranch. Knox is a brother of one of A's tenants, curiously enough. Duncan's parents live at Glen of Craigilon(?), near Turriff.

In Lady Aberdeen's perspective Chinese cooks and servants were an indispensable part of life in B.C. In fact she could not see how the British Columbia folk could get on without the Chinese. They were seen everywhere and in every domestic capacity. They were much better than girls from the old country who tended to be very selective over what they would or would not do. They could get "high wages" ($12 to $20 a month), but their general tone was not impressive. Although the Chinese themselves did not come cheap they dominated the domestic labour market as employers preferred them to girls who were not always "sensible."[7]

If Lady Aberdeen had reservations about the performance of young girls as servants she had a much wider view of the attributes which the average settler should possess. She thought that the Okanagan would suit either labourers or men with a little capital. The first group should have about £500 with which they could buy 20 acres of land, erect a small house, plant some seedlings and support themselves until the fruit begins to bear in sufficient quantity. This would take four to five years for apples, but other fruits or crops would begin to yield before them. The fruit grower would find the whole process of planting, pruning and generally nurturing his seedlings a "delightful occupation." Some college graduates, destined for the learned professions, had taken up fruit farming. The only advice, however, that she gave to the labourers was to save their high wages and learn the ways of the country. She very much hoped that the Okanagan would attract a good class of settler so that the district would offer a home of "good influences and high tone."[8]

Certainly the climate should offer some appeal. She and her family enjoyed it and it so suited the older residents of the valley that they "seem never to have found need for a doctor." It was a perfect Indian summer while they were at the Guisachan at the end of October, although she understood that in the winter the temperature could fall below zero for about six weeks and that the two months of summer could be very hot and ridden with mosquitoes. But all in all it was a very satisfactory climate.

Possibly because of the acquisition of the Coldstream, Lady Aberdeen did not describe any further visits to the Guisachan over the next four years. She noted, however, in her entry for October 20, 1895, that the fruit trees had not prospered because of the alkali in the soil and that it was still far from paying its way. Interestingly she observes with warm approval the first beginnings of a co-operative movement amongst the pioneers and mentions a visit to the Mission:

Sunday October 20th, 1895. Guisachan B.C.

We came on here from Sicamous on Friday. We are glad we

came down here, as we have found there is a good deal to arrange and re-organize. Morrison, the new overseer and his wife an O. & U. mother, whom we recommended to the Self-Help Society for Emigration three years ago, and whom we have imported from Manitoba this year, are doing very well—steady hard-working conscientious people, very anxious to cut down all expenses. He is from Inverness-shire. Most of the fruit-trees having done badly here because of the alkali in the soil, some new efforts must be made in other directions to make the place pay which it has been very far from doing so far. Professor Robertson recommends dairy cows and hogs—and both are to be tried. Mrs Morrison is a good dairymaid and we have been using her butter all the time at Coldstream. We are bringing Louisa Tremaine from Manitoba (one of the Ivy Cottage girls) to be trained under her. She is also very keen on poultry, and as eggs sell well, never less than 15 cents, and as both they and poultry are needed, we shall do a little in this way. The old Macdougal poultry-house is full of lice and vermin, and offers no protection against skunks, so it is to be burnt and a new plain little house built—also a small dairy and a piggery with movable troughs after a patent of H.E. suitable for winter use. There is a great demand for hogs now at the mines. The cows we bought at New Westminster and the little Ayrshire calf from Regina are to come here.

The people about here are moving in the direction of co-operation amongst the farmers, and the account of the success of Horace Plunkett's Irish Agricultural Association, which he has just sent me, comes in just a propos. They have formed a Farmers Union and a Shippers Union and are sending an agent up to Kootenay and to Calgary to open up the market and are thinking of sending a train full of vegetables and grains to warehouse and sell during the winter—they are also agitating about the rates and have already obtained some redress. H.E. has been v. busy going about amongst them all, encouraging them and gathering all the information he can. I have jotted down the names of those we have seen elsewhere. There are a number of educated young Englishmen here who have bought small farms and who are beginning to have hope, although money is still very short with them. There is Mr Stirling, who was in the navy, who has money and is v. keen about farming; Mr Lysons, the nephew of Gen. Sir D. Lysons and Mr Hobson his partner, both very gentlemanly young fellows; two young Roses, grandsons of Rose of the *Inverness Courier*; two young Fitzmaurices, grandsons of Mr Gladstone's rector at Hawarden; Mr and Mrs Pridham, tiresome grand people; Mr and Mrs

> Crozier, a nice old Cumberland man; Mr and Mrs Crichton, a happy looking young couple and so on. We have been advocating the formation of a Club on H. H. Club lines and A. guarantees the rent of an empty store as a reading room for the winter—and we think the idea will take shape. We are much interested by a visit to Father Cornelier at the Mission, who is very clever at all sorts of dodges for feeding his wild cattle and making them fat on hay only and then getting a good price for them. He is a modest young man and has only lately been put in charge here after missionary work amongst the Indians. We have been twice to Presbyterian service to-day—this morning at Kelowna and this evening at the pretty little church at Benvoulin which H.E. helped to build. Both services taken by Mr Mackay, a pathetic looking starved, wizened, little missionary—it was his first Sunday—he preached the same sermon twice. H.E. spoke at the end this evening about Elijah and service for others and told them about the idea of the Club.

The failure of the Guisachan and, as we shall see the Coldstream, to pay their way led Lord Aberdeen to ask several "experts" in succession for advice on how to put matters right. The first of these was his solicitor in Edinburgh, George A. Jamieson, who went to the Okanagan in 1892. In his report of November 16, 1892, he thought that while the price of $10,000 was right, too much had been spent on various improvements. "I am afraid that Mr. Eustace Smith, the manager, has rather encouraged than checked the not unnatural feeling that an English earl is fair game." He approved of the appearance of the new house, but complained that no tenders were invited from tradesmen for the building of the house and no architect employed (as if such talents were in ample supply in a pioneer society). He thought Smith was not very practical, but that Frank Conkling was very good. Without him the place "would never have been carried on so well." Still, if the orchards were to flourish, a qualified "fruit cultivator" would have to be hired. The Guisachan's general management remained a problem. It had been bought mostly for Coutts Marjoribanks, but he was essentially interested in cattle and was not "the man to sit down to cultivate apples and pears or hops." Mr. Mackay, who had bought it for Lord Aberdeen, should have appreciated this point and not recommended it. But then he claimed that Mr. Mackay himself had land in the vicinity of Guisachan and, worse, "a saloon on the roadside which I feel sure is full of risk to anyone residing all the year round at Guisachan." Nonetheless he was "generally greatly pleased" with his short visit, thought the Guisachan to be a good investment and indeed considered that Lord Aberdeen should have bought the nearby Knox Ranch, rather than the Coldstream.[9]

Two years later, in December 1894, Thomas Cunningham who was a member of the Board of Agriculture of the B.C. Government paid the Guisachan a visit. In his report of December 5, 1894, he praised the ranch: "The people who (condemn) it as unfit for anything but a hog ranch [which it became by 1896] do not understand it at all." It was true that many of the "fruit trees had done badly," but this was mainly due to the careless and reckless way they had been planted. He had never seen such disregard for the interests of the "owner as is manifested here on every hand... I feel indignant and vexed at the wrong done your Lordship." Still he was optimistic that they would recover from their bad start and yield fruit. Besides the ranch was well suited for corn, clover, timothy and potatoes. Mr. Cunningham advised Lord Aberdeen not to sell the Guisachan. There were not too many large bodies of land available "where the climate is as good." In drawing invidious comparisons with Vernon he said that when "we left (Kelowna) today it was warm and pleasant with hardly any trace of snow, but when we arrived at Vernon there were at least three inches and sleighs running in all directions with people clothed in wraps and ulsters and complaining of the cold snap. Mentally I added 20% to the value of the Kelowna district for climate."[10]

A less optimistic assessment of the Guisachan was made a year later in 1895 when Mr. William Saunders of the Central Experimental Farm in Ottawa paid it a visit. He said that for their age it was obvious that the trees had not grown satisfactorily while many others had died. He believed that the problem lay in the fact that the land was too low and that the roots of the trees were submerged in a comparatively high water table for too long each spring. This also explained the failure of the hops whose roots under such conditions would decay and die. "I do not think it would be possible to make a fruit plantation a success under existing circumstances at Guisachan."[11]

A grandson of Lady Aberdeen, the fifth Marquess, would have agreed with Mr. Saunders. In a laconic but not unkind recollection of the purchase of the Guisachan and its eventual effect on the family fortune, he observed ninety years later that with its acquisition, they were just on their way "on this incompetent, visionary, benevolent road to financial disaster,"[12] forty years hence.

The Guisachan was acquired by the Cameron family in 1903 and eventually taken over by Paddy Cameron, who owned it and lived there until his death in 1984. Whatever the economics of the ranch, the Aberdeens while they had it were delighted with it. As Lady Pentland observed, it was a relief to abandon the cares of a big estate in Scotland and to enjoy the informality of a small house and the optimism of what they considered to be their fellow settlers. At the time when they first knew the Guisachan, if not later, they were also buoyed up by the prospects the fruit industry seemed to offer.[13] In her old age Lady Aberdeen wrote that while the Guisachan had long since been sold she was pleased to recall that she still had family ties with the district since her niece, Ishbel Surtees, the daughter of Coutts Marjoribanks, lived at the Mission with her husband and small son. The son was the late John Surtees. His widow, Ursula, plays an active part in the Okanagan Historical Society.

Notes

CHAPTER II

[1] Pentland, Marjorie Lady, *Bonnie Fechter*, B. T. Batsford Ltd., London, 1952, p. 92.

[2] Aberdeen, Lady Ishbel, *Through Canada with a Kodak*, White & Co., Edinburgh, 1893, p. 155.

[3] Aberdeen, Lady Ishbel, *More Cracks with We Twa*, Methuen & Co., 1929, p. 89.

[4] *More Cracks*, p. 88.

[5] *More Cracks*, p. 92.

[6] *Kodak*, p. 192.

[7] *Kodak*, p. 198.

[8] *Kodak*, p. 194.

[9] Jamieson to Aberdeen, November 16, 1892.

[10] Cunningham to Aberdeen, December 5, 1894.

[11] Saunders to Aberdeen, December 9, 1895.

[12] Gordon, Archie, 5th Marquess of Aberdeen, *A Wild Flight of Gordons*, Weidenfeld and Nicholson, London, 1984, p. 190.

[13] *Bonnie Fechter*, p. 97.

CHAPTER III

Vernon and the Purchase of the Coldstream

Mr. Saunders' report about the Guisachan might have cooled the Aberdeens' ardour about the Okanagan had it been prepared a few years earlier. As it was, its purchase simply whetted their appetite for more land. Within a week after their first visit to the Guisachan in October 1891 they gave instructions to Mr. Mackay to find them additional property. They had heard that Colonel Forbes Vernon was willing to sell the Coldstream Ranch near Vernon. Lady Aberdeen had done well in the summer of 1891 over the sale of their town house in Grosvenor Square. She had just built it for £48,000 and an Australian had offered her £65,000. Such profit could not be overlooked and she agreed to sell the house. She and Lord Aberdeen decided to put £50,000 of the proceeds into the 13,000 acres of the Coldstream Ranch. Lady Aberdeen told herself that if they chose to give up buying a London house such a fit of speculation would be quite justifiable. Besides, the Aberdeens agreed with many Vernon residents that the prosperity of the area was being hampered by the refusal of Colonel Vernon to sell in lots any part of his ranch. If they bought it they could divide up part of it into smaller lots.[1]

A detailed account of how the deal was actually transacted still exists. In a letter of January 25, 1894 to his lawyers in Vancouver, Col. Vernon recalled that he (and his brother Charles) had acquired in 1863 some of the land on which the ranch was located. He decided to sell it in 1889 at a price of £40,000 for 1,000 head of cattle and 12,500 acres of land. A Mr. Wilson of Dublin expressed an interest in buying it, but the deal never materialized. The following year he withdrew it from the market because the Shuswap and Okanagan Railway was under construction. It could be to his advantage to hang on to it. Indeed he bought more land and more cattle. In October 1891, (by which time he was also provincial Minister of Lands and Works) he was approached by Mr. Mackay who explained that Lord Aberdeen wanted more land in the Okanagan. Mr. Mackay thought that only Tom Ellis' ranch at Penticton or the Coldstream would be suitable. Of the two he preferred the Coldstream because it was better suited for fruit and hops which were "much more profitable than raising cattle." Col. Vernon claimed that he had increased his price from £40,000 to £60,000 because land values had risen. Mr. Mackay argued that Ellis was only asking £50,000 for his ranch and in the end Col. Vernon agreed to accept the same price for the Coldstream. Lord Aberdeen was to pay £10,000 down with the balance over two years at 6%. "The whole transaction was commenced and concluded in less than an hour."[2]

In his report of the purchase on October 31, 1891 Mr. Mackay said:

> I have this day bought from the Hon. F. G. Vernon his ranch containing upwards of 13,000 acres (believed to be 13,500) together with about 2,000 cattle, about 70 horses, implements, pigs, furniture, crop, hay and everything movable on the ranch. I think it is a very reasonable price; he held out hard for $250,000 but I stuck to £50,000 which is only $241,000. He has sold no cattle this year so that interest for the money will come in beforehand by selling about 400 or 500 head of cattle. He has spent this year, as he shewed me by his books, about £3,000 in buying in extra cattle. He only used to have 1,000 head.
>
> Mr Vernon says it will keep 3,000 head of cattle easily. He has sold 300 tons of wheat; the whole produce of the year is still on the farm except that.
>
> I have made the formal entry to the property to be on 1st December so as to give you time to arrange about the payment of the £10,000 but practically you are to have immediate possession and this is very important because you might get a large sum at once from the usual cost of cattle not yet sold. Mr Vernon told me that there are about 100 fat cows to be sold for beef as they are not

> fit to carry calves longer, and younger ones are coming up to take their place. Mr Vernon was very sorry that he had not sold these, as it is at this time that they are usually sold, because he said that he would have that money (about £4,000) and the £50,000 as well! If we had been a month later this would have been the case. . . . I have no doubt whatever the ranch will yield more than 6 per cent. He assures me it will keep 3,000 head of cattle.[3]

Mr. Mackay told Lord Aberdeen that he was now the owner of the finest ranch in British Columbia. Financially, the Aberdeens had ample reason to think otherwise over the years that followed. The agreement of sale itself was the subject of protracted correspondence between solicitors and threats were made of court action. Curiously, the Aberdeens themselves did not first see their property until 1894—three years after they bought it and after they returned to Canada upon Lord Aberdeen's appointment as Governor-General in 1893. However, as with the Guisachan they had the benefit of the reports of their Edinburgh solicitor, Mr. George Jamieson and of Mr. Thomas Cunningham of the Board of Agriculture in Victoria. Both visited the Coldstream in 1892. The correspondence between Mr. Jamieson and Col. Vernon's solicitors in 1893 also sheds some interesting light on the problems of the Coldstream and broader social and economic factors in the North Okanagan at the time.

In the dispute over the purchase of the Coldstream, there seemed to be four principal issues at stake: the price itself that was paid for the ranch; the role of Mr. Mackay and other individuals in advising Lord Aberdeen; the number of cattle, and the quality of management.

Mr. Jamieson thought that as a speculative investment the Coldstream was a fair purchase. It was well supplied with water and had two large meadows "of exceptional utility." Still, in what seems to be a contradiction in terms, he believed that Lord Aberdeen paid far too much for it.[4] Mr. Cunningham also told him that he "had paid an enormous price for the estate and much more than was necessary . . ."[5] Naturally Col. Vernon, as the seller, thought otherwise. He believed it a "fair price" at the time, but observed that land values had declined not only in the Okanagan, but elsewhere. It is true that he asked £60,000 for it when Mr. Mackay approached him, but within an hour he accepted £50,000. This was the valuation of the property that he had put on his books a year before Mr. Mackay's offer and thus it could not be said that he had insisted on a high price just because the offer came from Lord Aberdeen.[6] Whether this is so or not, an attempt to get a high price for a piece of property would not be a sin in itself. After all the Aberdeens, by their own admission, would not have been able to buy the ranch if they had not done very well in the sale of their town house in London.

The supposedly high price raised the question of whether Lord Aberdeen was badly advised. Mr. Cunningham, in a thundering broadside, said that "the real estate agents of B.C. are little more than a set of pirates who have inflated prices and involved many people in serious loss." He believed that there has been "much conspiracy and downright dishonesty in evolving the schemes of your Lordship's investments in the neighbourhood and I know of my own personal knowledge that the conspiracy is not yet ended."[5]

Mr. Jamieson was more precise but perhaps not more accurate in pointing the finger at Mr. Mackay for not being a disinterested party in the transaction. He said that he had a "large interest in the Okanagan Improvement Company which controls Vernon and its whole surroundings." It was formed well before the railway was put through and "acquired the town site on very favourable terms." It had a capital value in 1892 of $365,000. Despite the apparent boom the "company is hard up. The main street is badly laid out; nothing is done to embellish it . . . nor to encourage the influx of visitors who would come from the damper climate of Vancouver and the coast to the fine dry warmth of Okanagan if the place were well managed." The acquisition of land by someone of Lord Aberdeen's name and influence would obviously benefit the company as "Vernon is plainly bound to be the centre of business in the Valley."[4] By 1892 at least Mr. Mackay's independence in handling Lord Aberdeen's affairs was further circumscribed by the fact that he had acquired some 300 to 400 acres nearer to Vernon than the Coldstream.

Mr. Jamieson noted that Mr. Mackay had accepted a commission not only from Lord Aberdeen, but also from Col. Vernon if the sale went through. He was in a sense serving two masters.[7] This was true. He had received $3,750 from Lord Aberdeen and $6,000 from Col. Vernon. He had not told Lord Aberdeen about the latter sum before he concluded the transaction, but he did return to him $1,250 after the event because of the fee received from Col. Vernon. Mr. Jamieson had accused Col. Vernon of paying Mr. Mackay to defraud Lord Aberdeen, but in reply Col. Vernon argued that when selling property he had always had to pay a commission.[8] Mr. John Campbell, Lord Aberdeen's lawyer in Vernon, said he did not believe there was collusion between Mackay and Vernon.

Mr. Jamieson considered that the principal problem was that the cattle were not properly counted and that Lord Aberdeen thought that he had bought more than he actually had. It will be recalled that Mr. Mackay reported that Col. Vernon used to have 1,000 head of cattle, that he spent in 1892 about £3,000 for additional cattle for a total of 2,000 and that he recommended that 400 to 500 should be sold more or less immediately. Col. Vernon's version is that on November 16 or 17, 1891 he and Mr. Mackay went with Mr. Marjoribanks and Mr. Eustace Smith, the manager of the Guisachan, to the Coldstream to hand over the ranch. "The animals were driven along and as good a count was obtained as is usually got when handling wild cattle . . . The cattle were in good order and more than the number mentioned (i.e. 300 steers and 100 fat cows) were fit for beef. . . . They were accepted by Mr. Mackay, Mr. Smith and Mr. Marjoribanks without a single word of protest."[2]

Mr. Eustace Smith, who was brought from the Guisachan to the Coldstream Ranch in 1892, did not sell the cattle that were ready for sale because he reportedly wanted more money for them than buyers were willing to pay. As it turned out the winters of 1892 and 1893 were very severe and a good many cattle died. Besides—which was another bone of contention—there was not enough feed on hand at the ranch to feed them and the Coldstream had to buy hay to enable its cattle to survive. A year after the sale Mr. Jamieson could not reconcile the number of cattle that he thought were bought with the number that existed when he was there in November. He suspected that Col. Vernon had deliberately overstocked the ranch before offering it for sale as Coutts Marjoribanks did not think it would normally carry the 2,000 claimed. He also argued that the cattle were thin and not ready for the market as claimed. In any case, despite the fact that few had been sold over the past year, there certainly were not 2,000 head on the ranch in November 1892. Mr. Jamieson was very suspicious that Wood, Vernon's manager, had sold or taken the hay and indeed laid a good deal of blame at his door for much of the apparent misrepresentation of the assets of the ranch.

Nonetheless, he admitted that after the purchase the "cattle were not well managed and their sale was injudiciously missed and a great many died owing no doubt to Mr. Marjoribanks and Smith being new in the country and having no one to advise them."[4]

Management was a major problem. Mr. Smith was replaced sometime before January 1894 by Mr. E. W. Kelly as the second manager. He, too, was critical of Col. Vernon and the way the sale had been handled, but he totally agreed that the way the place was managed after its purchase was the "laughing stock of the country. Mr. Smith, . . . whilst anxious to do his best for his employer was altogether too inexperienced in the business. Mr. Marjoribanks was supposed to look after the cattle because he had been amongst cattle in Dakota, (but) Mr. Smith and he were at variance at times . . . The mortality amongst the cattle must have been fearful for even the best run ranches lost heavily"[9] during the severe winters of 1892 and 1893. In December 1892, when the cattle were sold, the Coldstream accepted only $10 a head for them when Tom Ellis of Penticton would have offered $14. Col. Vernon said that he had understood that "the only thing upon which the management was entitled to any credit was the way in which the fruit trees and hops had been planted. That everything else had been grossly mismanaged from the inexperience of those in charge." Col. Vernon repeated this point when in summing up his position he said in a letter to his lawyers, "The whole subject is simply a matter of management. I did not guarantee any particular quantity of hay or fodder. I guaranteed nothing. There were the cattle: there was the ranche and everything upon it—I sold it as it was for a certain sum. Whether it would pay the purchaser or not was largely a matter of management..."[2]

Rightly or wrongly Mr. Jamieson felt sufficiently strongly about elements in the purchase of the Coldstream that he demanded some kind of satisfaction from Col. Vernon. He told him in 1894 that he wanted to avoid court action, but he suggested arbitration by "a mutual friend of high standing." Col. Vernon's solicitors rejected arbitration as they could see no reason for it. Presumably Col. Vernon then pressed for payment and possibly threatened to take Lord Aberdeen to court. Mr. Jamieson advised him to let Col. Vernon do so if he wished. He apparently did not take legal action, but while rejecting arbitration offered $3,000 as compensation. Mr. Campbell, Lord Aberdeen's lawyer in Vernon, advised him to accept the offer. Contrary to Mr. Jamieson's advice he thought "we would do badly if we took the matter to court." The $3,000 or "indeed any concession was sufficient." There was no evidence that Col. Vernon had misrepresented matters. Mr. Mackay had sought him out; Col. Vernon was not pressing the sale. He "asked a price" and Mr. Mackay agreed to give it to him "after he had inspected the property." He had acted hastily as he had often done in other transactions. "The second payment had been made without protest and it was late now to raise question."[10]

Lord Aberdeen had bought when land prices were high. Col. Vernon himself had been similarly caught and "had paid £17,000 for a property on one of the main streets of Victoria or about 20% more than he could get for it in 1894. Besides it does not bring in sufficient to pay its taxes and insurance, much less interest on capital." There may, however, have been another reason for this development in that the property in question was reportedly "nothing more nor less than an assignation house" according to Mr. Kelly. After Col. Vernon owned it "he tried to make it a respectable block, but he could get none to take rooms in it and it is still practically empty."[9]

What is the truth of the matter over the purchase of the Coldstream ranch? Mr. Campbell possibly came the closest to it in saying that Col. Vernon had, in pursuit of his own interests, asked what became a high price and that Mr. Mackay had accepted it. There was ample chance to inspect the property. Lord Aberdeen had commissioned him to find land and in a matter of this kind it was perhaps unjust to suggest as Mr. Jamieson did, that Col. Vernon set out to defraud Lord Aberdeen. It may have been true that Mr. Mackay suffered from a conflict of interest through his association with the development company, but if Lord Aberdeen wanted a man of substance to act for him he would recognize that he would likely own property. The question of the two commissions is perhaps more disturbing, but while it might not be acceptable these days, it could have been then. It is, of course, interesting that Col. Vernon did not take the matter to court and that in the end he reduced the price by $3,000. This could suggest some feeling of guilt but, on the other hand, it may have been simply a desire to maintain a degree of goodwill. After all, the compensation only amounted to slightly more than 1% of the total sum involved. He would also have been aware of the fact that by the time he made his offer Lord Aberdeen had become Governor-General and that regardless of the merits of the case it would have been inappropriate to continue a quarrel with a man who was the Queen's representative in Canada.

Whatever misgivings Lord Aberdeen might have had about his purchase of the Coldstream he was still willing to buy another 315 acres to extend his property to Kalamalka Lake. It was called Kalamalka Ranch and was owned by Price Ellison, an early settler and landowner in the district who later became a member of the provincial cabinet. The land stretched from the Coldstream Creek up the south side of the valley and along a narrow peninsula that entered the lake. Mr. Cunningham was sent to inspect it in December 1894. He approved of it. "The land is all that can be desired and slopes beautifully to the lake with a southern aspect. The beach is accessible—all the entire shore line some half a mile." The land provided "by far the best site for a future residence" and further it was important that Lord Aberdeen own Coldspring (sic) creek. It would provide a ready source of water for garden and lawn and for protection against fire if need be. Ownership of the mouth of the creek would also be important "if fisheries to any considerable extent are developed on the shores of Long Lake . . ." The Ellison land was also more sheltered from the "cold storms of winter" than were the buildings at the Coldstream Ranch.

Price Ellison was asking $60 an acre for his land. Mr. Cunningham advised Lord Aberdeen to offer $40 or a lump sum of $13,000. He was sure that Ellison "needs the money as all of the other settlers of B.C. need it just now and he is sure to become more deeply involved later on." At a later point he advised Lord Aberdeen to offer only $11,000. Land values were always difficult to judge, but Mr. Cunningham thought a long view was important. After all when one compared the area of good land in proportion to the sea of mountains in the province "one is forced to the conclusion that some day the agricultural lands of B.C. will be exceedingly valuable. We are not buying for today or for ourselves, but our children. A country with such a climate will not be at a discount very long."[11]

The land was, in due course, purchased and it was decided that the Aberdeens' residence would be built upon it, presumably on a site on the slope leading towards Rattlesnake Point. The Aberdeens never lived there, but the property was given to Coutts Marjoribanks. He left the Coldstream Ranch in 1895 to return to England, but later came back to the Okanagan. If memory serves correctly it was abandoned in the Thirties, but purchased in the Forties by the late Dolph Browne, a fruit shipper. The house burned down on March 1, 1957. The land is now a subdivision.

Now that they had the ranch it remained for the Aberdeens to decide how to run it, how to sell part of it and what to produce. They were not short of advice on any of these scores. They initially intended to encourage fellow Scots to come out and help run the place. The first to be invited to do so were William and Catherine Middleton. Under an arrangement largely initiated by Lady Aberdeen and Mrs. Middleton and only reluctantly accepted by her husband, the Middletons, then in their early forties, arrived with their five children in June 1892. Mr. Jamieson, however, had doubts about bringing out such "mature" people. He obliquely suggested that William Middleton, who had his own farm in Scotland and who was meant to develop the dairy end of the ranch, did not much like participating in the running of a larger operation.[4]

A scheme to sell land to settlers was more successful. Mr. Jamieson proposed a plan whereby potential buyers would buy land over twenty years and live on it as tenants in the meantime. The Aberdeens did not think much of this idea because many of the Vernon people would take up land on these terms, but "would never be able to pay." Instead lots were put on the market in 1892 for direct sale by instalments. By November 1893 they had sold 900 acres including property in the northwest corner to the Middletons.

Mr. Cunningham was critical of the way the property was being subdivided. He noted that only about a third of the Coldstream's land was fit for cultivation and the very best of it was set aside for sale "at (such) extremely low prices" as $20 per acre. He advised Lord Aberdeen to withdraw from sale the plots set aside for 40 acre farms and indeed reacquire those already sold. Instead he should sell those at a greater distance. It was unwise to dispose of land right on Coldstream Creek as the buyers in time would prove a source of trouble.[12]

On the question of what to raise or produce Mr. Mackay apparently believed that Lord Aberdeen should sell the cattle at once "as he didn't think there was any money to be made raising cattle in the Okanagan" and that he should go exclusively into "fruit and hops." However, Mr. Jamieson, straying from his field of expertise as a solicitor recommended dairying.

Beef was too dependent on the railways and slack markets. "Butter and cheese can wait for markets."[4] Mr. Cunningham surprisingly agreed with him. In all his travels he had not seen such poor cattle as are found in the Okanagan Valley... "not a decent bull in thousands. Your herd is no exception." However, "the dairying market for butter and cheese is unlimited. There is not a single drawback to dairying... There is no branch of farming that pays better... There can be no possible risk in this undertaking."[12] This advice seemed a little misplaced if one considered that most of the early inhabitants of Vernon owned their own cows and that the nearest market of any size was at the coast, 350 miles distant.

Mr. Mackay's advice about fruits and hops carried the day and the management set about with a will to develop them. Lady Aberdeen recalled later in her diary on December 4, 1896, that the original plan had been to plant forty acres a year until three hundred acres had been reached, but it soon became clear that irrigation both for hops and for fruit was absolutely essential in the Okanagan and that the creeks on the ranch could not supply water in sufficient quantity to cover such an area. Besides, an undated statement estimated that it would cost $64,000 to erect the necessary kilns to handle the hops from simply half that acreage. By 1896 they had only forty acres with plans to add another sixteen the following year. They could, she thought, produce hops at 7¼¢ per lb. In 1893 they received 16¢ per lb., but in 1894 only 13¢. Although this would seem a fair mark-up she described such prices as low since at one point hops had sold at $1.00 a lb. The forty acres produced about forty tons which at the lowest price of 13¢ would have brought $10,600.

By 1894 the Aberdeens had planted about 100 acres in fruit including strawberries and raspberries. The trees produced their first crop of twenty tons in 1896 and their third crop of fifty tons in 1898. It was sold at 2½¢ a lb. which would have worked out at around $2,500. All of this seemed a discouraging return. Mr. Jamieson had estimated that immediate financing at the Coldstream called for £64,000.[4] Whether or not this sum was spent is doubtful, but the annual expenditure of the Aberdeen resources was around $25,000 to $30,000. A total of $35,000 had been spent on the Guisachan alone in planting trees and hops. It is difficult to discover the reason for such outlays. Presumably it could not have been labour. In 1894 the Coldstream Ranch only employed fourteen men and general help was reportedly available at $200 a year plus food and accommodation because "there are thousands of men on this coast who are on the point of starving."[11] But whatever the cause the Coldstream Ranch continued to be a great drain on the financial resources of the Aberdeens. This did not, however, stop them from enjoying their visits nor taking pleasure from the development of the area.

Notes

CHAPTER III

1 *Bonnie Fechter*, p. 93.
2 Vernon to Messrs. Davis and Cassidy, January 25, 1894.
3 Mackay to Lord Aberdeen, October 31, 1891.
4 Jamieson to Aberdeen, November 16, 1892.
5 Cunningham to Aberdeen, December 4, 1894.
6 Vernon to Wood, July 4, 1894.
7 Jamieson to Vernon, October 26, 1893.
8 Vernon to Jamieson, January 25, 1894.
9 Kelly's comments on Vernon's letter of January 25, 1894.
10 Campbell to Jamieson, December 11, 1894.
11 Cunningham to Aberdeen, December 11, 1894.
12 Cunningham to Aberdeen, December 22, 1894.

CHAPTER IV

Life at the Coldstream

The Aberdeens first saw the Coldstream in 1894 when they made their third trip (and first as the vice regal couple) to Western Canada. In her *Journal* Lady Aberdeen expressed their delight with it. Amongst other things she described the hop picking by the Indians, spoke of the Aberdeens' decision to sell some of their land to settlers and mentioned some of those who had already arrived.

Coldstream B.C., October 30th 1894.

We have had a truly delightful time at Coldstream for the past ten days, though even there we have not found any spare time going a-begging. The scenery is lovely much of it reminding us of bits of Guisachan & Affric [in] Inverness-shire but quite apart from that there is a wonderful charm in feeling that one is once more on one's own domain & that one need not ask permission from the Government before moving a plank or ordering a plate or a duster. And then it is the first time that we have been en famille absolutely since we came to Canada, for Capt. Urquhart & Mr Erskine went off into the mountains on a big-game expedition—Mr Kelly, Mr Walker & Mr Ord turned out of the house & went to the men's house & A, Marjorie, Archie & I were left in undisputed possession. And we have enjoyed every moment of the time to the full, & feel as if we had regained our individuality, which was fast being worn away altogether into a machine likeness whose whole raison d'être consisted in receiving addresses & visiting institutions.

Marjorie has recorded our doings day by day (see below) so I will not repeat what she has reported very accurately, but merely jot down a few general impressions. To begin with, we quite agree that the beauty of the valley was not at all over-rated. The near hills on which the bunch grass used to grow look brown & barren at first, but one gets rather to like the peculiar colour & ridges. The more distant hills are broken & irregular in form & many are well wooded. The part of the estate bordering on Long Lake is most picturesque, & the disposition of the hills & water reminds us of part of Affric & Benevian. There is a delightful site for a shooting-lodge overlooking the lake & commanding two lovely views—this would be about 3 miles from the present farm buildings. It remains to be considered whether it might not be well to part with our fishing house in New Brunswick [*Richmond*] & come here instead in the summer. It would be beautifully out of the world, we could be quite by ourselves, & certainly it seems as if H.E. should come here every year during these early years when there is so much to be seen to & when the success depends so much on a watchful eye on all departments. Our coming here now has been a great relief to the manager, Mr. Kelly. We are very pleased with all we have seen & heard of him. He is very much in earnest over his work & is very business like, & the people of the district have found out that he cannot be taken in & his determination that H.E. shall be fairly dealt by & not be bled is doing good. He has got the prices for provisions for the whole district lowered by making a firm stand against the imposition of the merchants of Vernon. He got the list of prices from the Coast & then said he would pay 10% on these but no more—or he would get them straight from the coast—& so they have come down for all the people. Then too he seems to be dealing nicely with the new settlers who have come in & bought fruit-lots from us, paying by instalments. These settlers are of a very good class. Mr Abbott, his mother & two sisters, the son of an English clergyman, Mr & Mrs Spicer, cousins of Captain Spicer in the Guards; Mr Streatfield, a connection of Mr Streatfield who married Florence Anson; Mr Turner, the partner of the latter, a very gentlemanly looking young fellow; Mr & Mrs Venables with their children connection of Archdeacon Venables (they had been in the North West for some years, then went home for their children's education & have now settled here); Mr & Mrs Webster & a younger brother Webster (very superior people, who have travelled about a lot & have finally picked this as the choice place); Mr & Mrs Denison—well-read man, & working his place very well, Mr & Mrs Hall.... These ought to make a good nucleus for the future—but of course they all have to wait for returns from the fruit & the waiting is a bit hard.

But we have a lovely valley to divide up into similar 40 & 50 acre lots, with some pasture if desired—$30 per acre is the lowest price that has been paid. But we ought to get in time a really high-class little community here....

> Meanwhile we have every hope that the place will do well with our own crops of fruits & hops. Mr Kelly, who is generally a pessimist, says that he believes that it will pay back both the purchase money & also all that has been expended on it many times over. Meanwhile this is a bad year—a wretched bad year all round, including hops. Last year we got 16 cents per lb. for our hops. This year we are receiving only 13 cents & that is high for this year. Over in Washington Territory they are only getting 5 or 6 cents, so that many growers have just left them standing to save the expense of picking. Our hop-picking is a very picturesque sight from all accounts. The Siwash Indians arrive, tents & all & settle down for a holiday time at the picking. It is work that just suits them & they do it far better than either white people or Chinese. Big boxes are given to them numbered, & for each boxful they get $1—some get as much as $20 or $30 enough to keep them through the winter. At night they light their fires & dance & sing & amuse themselves & present a weird appearance. The danger was that the hotel-keepers in Vernon might get hold of them & make them spend their money in drinks, although it is against the law to supply any Indian with spirits. Mr Kelly however arranged only to pay them at the end & had a special constable sent to look after them & all went well.

Lady Aberdeen commented later that they only once had trouble with Indians they had hired. Apparently to secure enough hop pickers they hired some Indians from the state of Washington. They came armed with pistols which they shot off in races with the Canadian Indians. Thereafter they decided not to hire any American Indians. The B.C. Indians were generally accompanied by their old priest, Father Marzial. She thought that most of the priests who worked amongst the Indians in B.C. were Belgians. They had devised a system of pictures for teaching purposes and even published a magazine which used them as a medium of instruction.[1]

Her entry for October 30, 1894, continued about the contrasting fruit prospects for fruit at the Guisachan and the Coldstream, the somewhat premature building of a jam factory in Vernon and the staff at the Coldstream:

> We have now fifty acres in hops between Coldstream & Guisachan, & can produce therefore about fifty tons. The hops at

Coldstream are perfectly clear of hop-lice. Those at Guisachan are not, being so surrounded with brush, but nevertheless they are fine plants there too, with the exception of some diseased ones which were sent us by Wolff, the man from whom Cathy recommended us to purchase plants. Twenty-five cents per lb. is what we *want* to get, & then the hops would pay all our working expenses of both places. This is by no means an impossible price—they have been very much higher than that. We should like some big brewery to consent to deal with us direct instead of through agents & to give us instructions as to how they would like them dried etc. For on this point opinions differ. Last year they were supposed to be over dried, being dried at a temperature of 150° for 16 hours. This year they were dried for some twenty or thirty hours at 125° the lowest temperature which the hop expert says will dry them. We have a fine new hop kiln, with the newest self-feeding pressing machine etc.

Then the fruit orchard at Coldstream looks well—we have 100 acres planted. Apples will be our greatest stand-by. Pears do not do so well except one or two varieties, but cherries, plums & all the smaller fruits & all sorts of vegetables do magnificently. We are expecting some of our apple-trees to begin bearing next year. There is at present an illimitable & ever increasing demand for apples in the North West & in *this* province alone $15,000 worth of fruit was imported last year. For the smaller fruit, strawberries, raspberries etc. we had a ready market at 10¢ a lb. at Vernon this year without going further. The jam-factory which H.E. put up in Vernon & which is a remarkably fine building, is not thus likely to be wanted yet awhile. He put it up in fulfilment of a promise to the people so as to assure them of a market if they took to growing fruit, but there are many old-timers & they are slow to move. However when the time comes, there will be openings for making jam, canning fruit, evaporating apples, & pickling vegetables. The miners want a great quantity of evaporated apples, & they get them all from the south at present.

The fruit at Guisachan is a failure, owing to alkali & the ground being so near a level with the lake that the water comes in the roots. And so it has been a big loss to plant all those trees down there. We shall probably have to turn it mainly into a pig ranch combined perhaps with dairy. Pigs pay very well & there is a good market for them at Victoria. We are going to experiment on feeding 40 pigs with wheat to see if the return is as good as is stated from Mr Armour's trial, whereby he estimated that wheat fed pork brought in 75 cents for the wheat instead of the ruination 26 cents which it is now going for. Our 800 cattle are only a loss & after entailing wages & food all winter sell for less than the hay itself would have fetched. We are going to get rid of them therefore as soon as possible only keeping enough for beef. Our two hundred horses are another opening but they need improving & the market for them has to be sought.

Poultry also ought to help, as there [*are*] but few people bringing up poultry in the province & 25 or 35 cents per dozen can be depended on in Vernon. In Victoria 60 to 75 cents per dozen is the price for eggs, but then the freight to the Coast is prohibitive. The freight on fruit is double what the duty is on fruit coming from the States & for every car load of cattle holding about twenty, $125 is charged.

This year there will be a big deficit in the income as compared with the expenses. And Mr Kelly does not think it possible to reduce the expenses consistently with assuring the ultimate success of the place, a success of which he is confident. But it needs patience & unceasing vigilance—& shrewdness too in looking out for a market.

We have a very nice staff of men to all appearance. Will the foreman from Methlie. Furness the fruit superintendent, a cousin of Harry Furness's, Mr Fitzmaurice one of the two young men recommended by Mrs Gladstone, the grandson of a former Hawarden rector. Brightland etc.—Also Mr Walker who acts under Mr Kelly & Mr Ord who keeps the books.

We had two evening services at the house like those at home, to which they all came, H.E. taking the lead, & they liked it. We also got a reading-room started at Vernon for all the young men who loaf about, H.E. giving his butcher's shop for it.

Here follows Marjorie's journal while we were at Coldstream.

There are two lengthy entries of Marjorie Gordon which are included in the *Journal* for October 1894 and, a year later, for September and October 1895. They provide an account of how the younger members of the Aberdeen family enjoyed their holidays in the Okanagan and of the people they met and knew. She spoke of a hunting party led by Sir Peter Walker which killed five "grizzly bears" one of which was "seven feet long" and of her own success on a different foray in killing a chipmunk "by shooting it between the ears." Her brother, Archie, is credited with various woodpeckers, blue jays and magpies, but both realized that they could not go too far afield as they had once "got into trouble for being late." She did not specify the trouble, but it must have made them conscious of parental interest in their whereabouts since on a subsequent day "Archie several times answered a crowing cock which he thought was Mother." They often went for rides "towards Long Lake" and one afternoon the family all drove to the "Meadows belonging to Father up the Valley about five miles." They were about "1040 acres" in area with a good deal of bush. The road went through "lovely woods of birch and fir with a little burn running along. It was just like Scotland; Father compared it to Balmoral." Two miles further on they came to "Lumbie, a small village" and in another two miles "we came to the Upper Meadows." On their return they stopped at the hotel at Lumby and passed by the Presbyterian church "which was built by the people themselves. . . . The English church people use it, too." On another occasion she painted "what they call here the Oregon Grape vine. It grows in gardens at home. I think it is called larrishmus and has shiny leaves like holly and blue berries."

Marjorie Gordon mentioned various callers at the ranch—Mr. Wood, the Methodist minister, Mrs. Abbot and her two daughters and "Father Marzial, the old priest in charge of the Indians." On another day the Abbots, Mr. and Mrs. Denison and Mr. Turner came to "church service" at the ranch while Mr. Fitzmaurice, with whom she rode on occasion, is recorded as having ridden the five miles into Vernon in 20 minutes in order to put some letters on the train. During a visit to Kelowna they drove to the Rose's, "two brothers from Inverness who have a fruit farm" and then to the Pridham's. As they went down the lake on the *SS Aberdeen* Lady Aberdeen "sketched the beautiful scenery."

From Vernon the Aberdeens proceeded to the Coast for several days. In her *Journal* Lady Aberdeen said that she liked Victoria "very much. The scenery around is lovely, the climate good and healthy and the town appears to us very liveable. We have also met a good many nice people. The tone is decidedly English."

On their return East they stopped at Kamloops and Salmon Arm:

November 15th 1894. Salmon Arm, B.C.

A lovely day for our function at Kamloops though very cold & reminding us distinctly that we have left the mild regions of the coast & shall now have to look forward to winter ways for the next five months. The Mayor (Mr Lee) Mr Mara M.P., Judge Walkem, & Dr. Farrer & Mr Marpole boarded our train at 10 a.m. & we delivered ourselves over for the usual programme. The station was gaily decorated with evergreen arches & bunting & coats of arms & a number of vehicles were in readiness for the state drive, including a team of tiny Shetlands for Archie's express benefit.

1. Civic address outside the Town Hall on a specially prepared platform with a very prettily designed arch. A somewhat chilly ceremony in the keen air, but H.E. descanted happily on his experience & aspiration as a fruit grower.

2. Then came the school-children with their address & the answer. A little girl Una Mackintosh, presented Marjorie with a nugget of gold made up as a brooch.

3. Drive to Old Man's Home—for the province which is nearing completion. An institution which is much needed for broken down & destitute old pioneers. A nice building.

4. Hospital—Miss Potter matron—12 beds.

5. Industrial School for Indians taught by sisters. Very good. Both boys & girls recited dialogues, sang & showed results of needlework instruction with great credit after 1½ year's schooling. Father Lejeune the great man here, & a great authority on B.C. Indians. H.E. presented prize—& I one for needlework.

6. Address from Indians & Father Lejeune interpreter. They are v. advanced Indians here & support themselves almost altogether by agriculture.

7. Drive through town, which has greatly increased since we were here last. It is a railway divisional point & most of the inhabitants are connected with the Railway. Mr Marpole, the divisional Supt lives here, & is evidently deservedly popular. Kamloops boasts a Chinatown & a jap-house & all the Chinese turned out to greet us in their best clothes.

We left Kamloops by freight train about 2 & halted at Shuswap in hopes of a sketch, but the light was waning & when I tried to paint, the water in my paint-brush froze as I painted. So we came on to here to Salmon Arm. Mr Erskine & Mr Kelly joined us here & we had a long Coldstream talk. Mr Erskine preceded us from Victoria in order to go over accounts with Mr Kelly.

The ten day visit of the Aberdeens to the Okanagan in 1894 was followed by one of six weeks' duration in September and October 1895 less a ten day trip to the Coast and the Kootenays. To check on arrangements for their longer stay they stopped at the Coldstream for a few hours in mid-August while travelling from the East to Vancouver and Victoria:

Thursday August 15th. Victoria, B.C., Government House

Here we are at last after three weeks travelling & it is very delightful to be at rest & all together again by ourselves in a comfortable house amidst lovely surroundings.

We journeyed all day on Monday from Field to Sicamous, where we stopped for the night. It is a lovely spot on the borders of Shuswap Lake & old Col. Forester, who won fame in the Chinese wars long ago, keeps a very good hotel, to which many sportsmen repair. Fear of mosquitoes however kept me pretty close to the car. On Tuesday morning at 7:30 we moved on to Vernon, which we reached soon after 10. Mr Kelly met us at the station—also little Beatrice Myott, who looks much stronger & quite pretty. She & Georgie Dallas were overjoyed at meeting one another & went off together hand in hand to talk over all things, past, present & future & Beatrice's coming wedding in particular.

We soon drove off to Coldstream, & were very busy planning arrangements for our stay there later on, H.E. devising various simple but comfortable alterations to the house, & going over the plans for the new stables. The old ones were burnt down about a fortnight ago from the explosion of a lamp & the whole thing was burnt down to the ground in about 10 minutes and unfortunately two of the horses were burnt too, these being two of Coutts old favourites, Harry & the roan. They would not come out & Harry ran back when pulled out. Happily the insurance covers the loss, & the new stables will be up in a month. All else looks well—hops & trees etc. & the outlook is much more promising than last year. It was very hot & the flies were v. bad. Mr Whyte of the C.P.R. & his boy, his friend Mr Irving of Toronto & his two boys, who had been out to Penticton, came out & joined us for a bit before we all went back to catch the 4 p.m. train. Beatrice too brought out her fiancé, who appears a pleasant respectable sort of man.

From Sicamous we journeyed right on to Vancouver, swaying & shaking violently on the way in the engine's successful but uncomfortable efforts to make up time & we arrived duly on time about 1 p.m. yesterday.

They returned from the Coast on September 5 by train (during which two favourite horses, Filbert and Atlas, were killed when a steam pipe burst in their boxcar) and set out to enjoy their holiday:

Thursday September 12th. Coldstream Ranch

Whilst we are here, I do not intend to keep my journal every day, for happily one day goes past very much as another, though each is full of quiet delight & interest. H.E. spends a good deal of time in his hop-yards, his orchards, or his farm, discussing arrangements & prospects with one & another, & every now & again takes a turn on his bicycle. The children do four or five hours of lessons every day, Dr Gibson coming out from Vernon (where he & Mr Campbell live at the Kalemalka Hotel) on his bicycle to give them two hours of Latin & Greek & physiology. With me they are [*reading*] Parkman's History, Dr Bourinot's Government of Canada, letter-writing, French, English & German poetry, the ordinary sort of lessons to learn & a Bible-lesson of course. They are very delightful children to teach, for they are so keen & see the point of everything. They ride with John Keddie most days & bicycle. I think there is a white horse, which I shall try to ride presently, but I am afraid of its not being strong enough for me & all the horses here are ugly & uninteresting. We have had a real evil lately with our horses altogether this year. Coutt's two old favourites refusing to be dragged out in the fire, Jim dying of influenza, & since we have been here, another young mare being seized with colic on her way in to Vernon & dying the same day. Our dear "Filbert" & "Atlas" have been laid to rest at the corner of the orchard, at the end of a path leading from house. They will be long remembered. People generally seem very sorry about it & Atlas had already gained a wide reputation for his wonderful beauty. People at Victoria used to come to the stable & ask to be allowed to see him. Poor John Keddie is quite disconsolate, & is as a nurse bereft suddenly of her charges. On top of this he has had a letter telling of a serious accident to his father in Scotland. He is a splendid hard-working little fellow & full of intelligence.

H.E. has cabled to Jim Power to try & find a new cob & send him out at once, & the C.P.R. undertake to bring it & Beechnut for H.E. over the Continent free of charge. Mr Jim has answered that he hopes to find an animal within the week. He found Atlas & knows exactly what we want. The C.P.R. authorities are much perturbed about the accident & have been making an enquiry into it, longing to hit upon some reason which would shift the blame from themselves—but it cannot be. The handle turning off the steam *was* turned off, it is true, but the fact of these cut off pipes rendering an accident possible ought not to have been overlooked. Mr Marpole, & Mr & Mrs Spencer, Supt. of Eastern Division with some ladies, were here one day—Sir Alfred Wills, the English judge & his daughter, & Mrs Cochrane from the Cochrane Ranch near Macleod lunched yesterday & went over the orchards & hop-yards & were delighted with the sight, much admiring the beauty & the luxuriance of the hop-vines.

Haddo & Dudley with Miss Wetterman & Mr Ferguson left us on Saturday travelling East in our own car under charge of Sergeant Rogers as cook & Frederick the under-butler.

They had a nice sight of Guisachan & drove up here next day by Long Lake thus getting a good view of picturesque part of the country. And then here they had time to see round the premises & the orchards & the hops & to go out on a little prairie-chicken shooting expedition with H.E. The two small boys were in a wild state of excitement over this & most willingly turned into beaters. Perhaps it is unfair to mention the finale when they rushed forward when the covey got up & so spoiled the sport. Nevertheless a brace was bagged. I think we all feel that these have been holidays to which we shall look back as having been eminently satisfactory in all ways—Haddo & Dudley sail by the *Numidian.* They were to make one halt on the way East at Brandon, & we gave them a letter of introduction there to Senator & Mrs Kirchhoffer, & they wired that they had a delightful day. They have the captain's cabin, & the second officer's cabin again, so will be v. comfortable & Haddo likes the Captain much. It seems really best if possible for them to come by the Canadian line, avoiding New York, troubles about baggage & being specially looked after. But the boats starting on Thursday by the Allan are not very convenient generally for school arrangements & exams.

The Indians have arrived to pick the hops & very pretty & picturesque they look; but of this & other ranch matters more next time. We are wholly engrossed with farming anxieties now & have forgotten Manitoba & all else. It has been v. wet the last two days for a wonder.

Tuesday October 8th 1895. Coldstream Ranch, Vernon, B.C.

My journal has had its promised holiday and so have its readers—to their great relief, I should imagine. . . . We have had a real "lovely time" as they call it—nearly five weeks now of absolute quiet. H.E. is intensely interested over his hops and fruit and farming operations and all is very promising for the future. It is a gloriously beautiful country as to scenery and climate and a perfect riding country. Miles and miles of soft roads. I found an old white horse, Prince, to carry me but he is not extra safe and I wish Mr Power had been able to find me a new "Atlas" in time. But he has not.

Notes

CHAPTER IV

[1] Aberdeen, Lady Ishbel, *We Twa*, Collins, London, 1925, p. 89.

1. Lady Aberdeen.

2. Adjacent to the boat dock at Kelowna.

3. Kelowna landing stage, *circa* 1894.

4. Okanagan Lake near Guisachan, B.C.

5. First residence at Guisachan.
6. Second residence.
7. Third residence.

8. Fourth residence at Guisachan.
PROVINCIAL ARCHIVES OF ALBERTA / E. BROWN

9. Guisachan Ranch.
PROVINCIAL ARCHIVES OF ALBERTA / E. BROWN

10. Hop gardens, Guisachan.
PROVINCIAL ARCHIVES OF ALBERTA / E. BROWN

11. *Aberdeen* sternwheeler, Kelowna, B.C.

12. Okanagan Lake, near Orr Ewing Point.

13. Postill Lake, now named Woods Lake.

14. Kalamalka or Long Lake and Woods Lake—overlooking the "railway" or what is now Oyama.

15. First passenger train to Vernon, October 14, 1891.
16. Vernon, 1894.

17. Kalamalka or Long Lake, Vernon, B.C. *circa* 1885.
PROVINCIAL ARCHIVES OF ALBERTA / E. BROWN

18. Coldstream Valley—Looking East.
PROVINCIAL ARCHIVES OF ALBERTA / E. BROWN

19. Coldstream Valley—Looking West toward the Commonage and what is now Middleton Mountain.

20. Coldstream Ranch.
PROVINCIAL ARCHIVES OF ALBERTA / E. BROWN

21. Buildings on the Coldstream Ranch.
PROVINCIAL ARCHIVES OF ALBERTA / E. BROWN

22. Cattle scene on the Coldstream Ranch, 1891.
23. Ploughing on the Coldstream Ranch, *circa* 1891.

24. Coldstream Water Wheel, 1885.
PROVINCIAL ARCHIVES OF ALBERTA / E. BROWN

25. Steam Shovel Crossing Flume Support Structure—Coldstream.

26. View down the Valley—Irrigation Flume.

27. Hop kilns at Coldstream Ranch, *circa* 1897.

28. Penticton, B.C., *circa* 1892.

Unless otherwise indicated the photographs are taken from the Haddo House archives.

CHAPTER V

A Visit to the Kootenays

After a month's rest the Aberdeens opened an indifferent Vernon agricultural show and met the Dominion Dairy Commissioner, who very much impressed Lady Aberdeen. They spent a few days at the Coast again including a "lively night" above a bar in New Westminster. They then proceeded to the Kootenays.

October 11th 1895. New Westminster, B.C.

This week has been a week of conflicting Agricultural Shows for us. Last year we promised to come to the "Royal" Show here this year. What was our Horror therefore when we found that our good Vernon folk had fixed theirs for the self-same days! Finally a compromise was arranged whereby H.E. was to open the home Show at Vernon on Wednesday and then come on straight here by the same afternoon's train. This was duly accomplished but it was disappointing to find the comparatively slight interest taken in the Vernon Show by the farmers around as indicated by the meagre collection of exhibits of grain and roots and fruit and vegetables in a district where all these products excel. They seem to be all discouraged by the high rates of the C.P.R. and the low prices and do not realize what good the advertisement of their goods at a Show at some expense or trouble to themselves will do them. There were some good apples however at any rate. H.E. opened the Show soon after 2, after inspecting the exhibits for which a building had been erected near the race-course about a mile or more away from the town. He gave his neighbours some good advice and was followed by Prof. Robertson, the Dairy Commissioner for the Dominion whom I have mentioned before in this journal in connection with his work in the Maritime Provinces and the Agricultural Conferences he organized there last year for H.E. to attend. He is a capital man, full of enthusiasm for his work and of real zeal for the development and up building of the country. He always finds means too to lift the principles and precepts about farm work on to a high plane, appealing to the moral as well as the material side of human nature. He puts the care and enriching of the soil as a duty imposed on every cultivator by God, and one which must be performed if the man is to die honest—he shows how care and kindness and thought both for the animals whom we rear for our own profit as well as to those who work for us gives the best results in all ways. He shows clearly how brains and a good education and thinking is necessary for farmers and then he gives an infinity of useful and practical hints not only about dairy and creamery work but about agricultural work in general and its outlook and how only "the best" of everything can hope to succeed in the present war of competition in all businesses and trades. H.E. had gone up with him to Guisachan on Monday for a meeting there which was well attended and which excited much interest. His speech at Vernon lasted almost till the hour for the starting of the train—4 p.m. So we could only take a hasty look at the stock and depart. Mr and Mrs Bostock were there, having driven over from Ducks. He is a young Englishman of means who is running in the Liberal interest for the constituency against Mr Mara, the present M.P. who was also there. Mr Bostock is very keen about the development of the Province and is spending a good deal of money—he has a ranch, has built a house in Victoria and has started the capital weekly paper *The Province.*

It was a v. shaky journey to Westminster....

Friday October 11th

Had a lively night, inasmuch as the bar was directly under my room. At 1:15 H.E. rang to ask the night porter when the hotel was shut up. "Not at all" was the answer. "When does the bar close." "Not at all, Sir." However it was further explained that this was only the case at the time of the Fair, when there was absolutely no beds available and when therefore the visiting young men were allowed the use of the bar room for the night. They certainly did use it, but happily the singing and shouting were so continuous that I was finally sung to sleep and woke only to hear the carousal being closed by God save the Queen shortly after 8 a.m. But as we are the guests of the city on this occasion, we must say nothing.

On October 12, 1895, the Aberdeens left New Westminster

for Shuswap and then Revelstoke where they caught another train to take them to the steamer that carried them down the Columbia River to the Arrow Lakes and Nelson. In her entry written at Nelson Lady Aberdeen told of the capacity of one John Kirchup for keeping order at Rossland and drew invidious comparisons between the situation there and just across the border in the United States where people "gash and shoot at one another without any let or hindrance":

Sunday October 13th. Shuswap

We dropped here early this morning and have had a beautiful quiet day. Such lovely weather too.

This afternoon walked to head of lake some 3 miles away. Found there a store kept by an old Scotsman Ross, who has been in this district for 30 years and who gave me some photographs he had taken. He had a company of young Finlanders who were receiving a newcomer from Finland in the shape of a bride who had been sent for by one of their number, Randes at Notch Hill. He left when she was 13 and he was 19, and now he sent her money to come over and the wedding is v. shortly to take place. She is living at the section-house now with John Nicholson and Mrs Nicholson, the foreman here, and we went to see them this evening, and gave the young lady a Union Jack brooch, with which she seemed delighted. Nicholson brought me down from the lake on a hand-car, a sort of trolley which runs on the rails and is what is called "pumped" along by hand. I have rather objected to this species of locomotion before, but was glad of the lift to-night. Mr Clark the station-agent and his Ontario wife still here—they gave us some apples.

October 15th, Nelson, B.C.

Yesterday morning early the East bound train picked us up at Shushwap, Mr Erskine and Mr Campbell at Sicamous where they had spent the Sunday under Col. Forrester's care, and Mr Mara, M.P. at Kamloops. This latter gentleman is acting as conductor and host during this trip, as he is the principal owner of the steamers plying on the river and lakes in this region.

We were deposited at Revelstoke soon after 11 and there the good people were kind enough to allow us to abide in peace for the few hours before the steamer left. It was a glorious day and the place was looking very pretty, with snow silvering the heights.

At 5 our car was attached to the little train which runs the 16 miles down to the Wigwam, whence the steamers start, and we were surprised to find so fine and well-equipped a boat. It is built on the same plan as the *Aberdeen*, only larger, with a large wheel in the stern. All the appointments and arrangements are good and should invite tourist traffic along a river and series of lakes the grandeur of which fairly surprised us. We had heard so much about the Kootenay district from a mining point of view and of the great prospects opening out in this respect, without ever hearing the scenery mentioned at all, that we were unconsciously prepared for a somewhat barren looking district. Instead of this, we have passed for hours through the most enchantingly beautiful country, looking its very best in the most perfect weather. At first the steamer makes her way for some twelve miles along the Columbia river and then passes into the Arrow Lakes. These seem more like a wide river than a lake and as you twine round the bays, most exquisite views are obtained of blue distances and ranges of mountains mostly clad with pine and larch. The latter in their autumn dress greatly augmented the beauty of the scene. Added to all this a cloudless sky, brilliant sunshine and waters of the deepest and most gorgeous blue.

We left the boat at Robson and came on here by train skirting the Kootenay river where there is supposed to be the most lovely trout fishing and some lovely falls, where they stopped the train for us to get out to admire and to photograph.

This place itself is very prettily situated in a nest in the mountains, overlooking the river. Affaric is the only place one can compare to what have seen to-day.

It is very pleasant too to be conscious of the sense of bien-aise and of coming prosperity—the address presented here on the steps of the hotel alluded to it and the countenances and expressions of the people betokened it. The normal population here is about 600, but there is a shifting population in connection with the mines and prospecting. Most of the miners have come from the U.S.A. and hitherto the capital invested here has been mainly American, but Mr Barnard has brought good news from England in announcing the formation of this syndicate said to be backed by the Rothschilds with £500,000 capital for developing mines in this district. He is up at Rossland now and we expect to see him on his way back to-morrow. We are sorry that our ignorance about the ways of the steamers and the days they start must prevent us from going to Rossland this time, for we cannot spare three days out of our precious remaining fortnight at Coldstream. But Rossland is a remarkable place. A year ago there were but two houses there—since then an American found a mine, tested the value of the ore (gold) with the result that it proved to be all that could be desired. Now there is a population of 2000 mostly from the other side of the line. These people, belonging as they do to a wild and lawless class, are accustomed to cut a gash and shoot at one another without any let or hindrance. But the moment they come into British territory they realize that "Aunt Peggy's laws" (this is their name for Her Majesty) are made to be obeyed—they drop their revolvers and are willing to be kept in order by one constable. This is actually the case at Rossland. There reigns one John Kirchup [*Kirkop*] formerly of Revelstoke; a big burly man with the air of authority in every look and gesture. If a man gets drunk and begins to make a row the word whispered "John Kirkup's coming" is sufficient to make the miscreant look round in terror and bolt if possible. He has not even a lock-up wherewith to uphold his authority; but it seems that his method is simply to lay his hand on the guilty one's shoulder with a word warning—"you'll get into trouble"—should this not suffice he takes him by the collar and gives him a shake and removes him into the road—the worst penalty is a night on the sofa in his office. A fight was imminent in a saloon a short time ago. Kirkup was sent for. "Come out into the road here and I'll give you five minutes." Soon one began to show he was the weaker. "Now, that's enough" said Kirkup, laying hand on them, "go home." And they stopped quarrelling and went. Our friend Mr Gordon told us some of these stories and Mr Mara has been telling us more. The remarkable thing is that he should be able thus to impose British law on people who fifty miles away utterly defy all restrictions. H.E. wrote him a letter to-day expressing our regret not to be able to come to Rossland, and thanking him in the name of the Queen, for the work he is doing in thus giving a good start to the town. Already a Presbyterian Church is built, in accordance with the forward policy of the Presb. Church, and Mr. Bordon and Dr Robertson were much touched by the heartiness of the gathering they had there when they opened it. A Methodist and an R.C. Church are following and probably an Episcopalian will soon come.

Here there are the four churches too, as usual. Sir Joseph Trutch, once Lt Governor of B.C. and a very well known man, came down with us to-day. He is the President of "The Silver King" the largest silver and copper mine in the whole Province and the only one in which British capital is invested. It has been worked rather sluggishly till lately, but the success of the Americans has woken people and there is a great desire in the district to see British capital coming to the front. A smelter is now being built for the Silver King and all looks bright.

H.E. has been having a long talk with Mr St Barbe, the editor of the paper here, who is a very intelligent young man. He says he hears there is an article in the *Saturday Review* casting doubt on the genuineness of the capital of the new syndicate which he is afraid will do harm. All the wise people in this country, including Sir William Van Horne, have no doubt as to the future here and show their faith by investing.

We took a tour round the chief stores of the town with Captain Fitzstubbs and H.E. endeavoured to lay foundations for future trade for our district. Success here for the mines means much for us as the miners must be fed and want the best of everything—beef and fruit and vegetables and grain. Already a beginning is being made. But freight rates have been against us, and although they are now lower, they are still high—for instance $9, per head for cattle from Vernon here—the chief butchers, Burns, and Purdee are ready at this moment to give $36, per head delivery here. H.E. is going to telegraph to see if we cannot send up a hundred or so. They would send a man to look at them. The chief merchant of fruit told us he could get apples from Washington Territory for 2½ cents per lb. including duty. I do not know if we can compete against this. We have been getting 5 cents a lb. for crab apples at Vernon and 2½ and 3 for other apples.

However this is evidently a grand market and H.E. enjoyed his chats very much.

Sir Joseph Trutch and Mr Mara dined with us at this nice clean comfortable hotel, managed by Mr Phair from New Brunswick. The maids look so neat and tidy, and Mr Phair actually met us at door and showed us up to our rooms as a matter of course.

Had a reception after dinner to-night of the rank and fashion of Nelson.

They then went on to Kaslo where they received a warm welcome even if Lady Aberdeen was distressed to note the presence of an American variety theatre "of the lowest type":

Wednesday October 16th. "S.S. Nelson" Arrow Lake

Our orders were to be ready to start by steamer for Kaslo at 8 a.m. and so we were, but the morning mist was so thick that the steamer had been detained, and we had to wait for half an hour. This was a special trip arranged by the directors for us, and so the boat had only just time to land her night passengers and take us on. As we embarked the mist was just rolling away from the mountains and the sun shining through making a most lovely effect with the autumn colours added to make all perfect. We have had another long day of matchless scenery seen under the most favourable circumstances and in the most faultless weather. And we felt very grateful to Mr Mara in not making up a party of his constituents to come with us and in not asking any ladies to "attend" me. Only Capt. Fitzstubbs, the Gov. Agent, Mr Mara, Mr Jowett and Captain Troop the Manager of the S.S. Co. And they left us very kindly alone except at meals, so we were free to sit on the deck and read and sketch and photograph or do nothing as we wished. While the mornings are cold, the sun for three or four hours in the middle of the day is exceedingly strong and hot. Our course lay through a narrow arm of the Kootenay Lake running direct East at first, and then N.E. up the lake at Kaslo. We stopped at Pilot Bay for half an hour or so to go over a smelter put up by an American Co., who are also working the Blue Bell mine. Mr Heindricks the manager much wanted us to go over to the mine some few miles away and a great deal of which can be seen right on the surface. But there was not time, and perhaps I did not regret this personally, for I fear I do not love the dirt and din of mines and smelters and all the break-neck places you are expected to go, with waggons and wheelbarrows of various minerals being emptied out all over the place unexpectedly. Having now been down a coal-mine, down a gold-mine, and over two smelters, I feel I have done my duty and hope that all future mines may be situated in such lovely surroundings, so that I may suitably make an excuse of wanting to sketch. H.E. however is becoming quite a convert to mining and its intricacies, and more especially in the great opening it evidently is going to give us farmer-folk. He made a bargain with Captain Gore to-day of this steamer to supply a friend of his with 20 tons of oats at $38 a ton. This gentleman has had to pay $41 up to now.

The authorities at the smelter give very glowing reports of the character of the metal which is being tested here—it is mostly silver and lead in this neighbourhood and gold and copper at Rossland. The Blue Bell mine is sending out 200 tons of mineral every day—that is silver and lead and some copper.

Opposite Pilot Bay a gentleman of the name of Balfour has built a private residence just because of the beauty of the place. And he is fully justified. This must be a very favourite resort with tourists some day and that before long with these comfortable and commodious steamers and good hotels.

We shall certainly advise all our friends to turn down here. And then the fishing is so good. It is a wonderful good fortune for the people of this district to have these wonderful water-ways—three chains of navigable rivers and lakes from North to South from 150 to 200 miles long connecting with the C.P.R. for Canada and the Northern Pacific for the U.S.A.—it makes everything very easy for the miners.

Kaslo is a mining town of the American type, and is still very much in the rough, with the streets all full of stumps. Poor little Kaslo, it has had many trials, a fire destroying nearly the whole town, and when it was but half built up again a flood and a tornado which all but swept it out of existence and which tossed about the little wooden houses like toys. But there Kaslo is and there it means to stay. It has about 900 inhabitants and a Mayor and Corporation which appears to be a doubtful blessing as they have licensed an American variety theatre of the lowest type, the only one of its kind in Canada, to amuse the miners. But the disgrace of it is felt, and some of the ladies spoke very strongly to me about it. Kaslo was very anxious to do the right thing to-day, never having had to deal with such a being as a Governor-General before, and moreover being desperately afraid of being outdone by Nelson. So it received us in grand style with dynamite salutes and prolonged discordant strains of "God save the Queen" by the band. We were then escorted by the Mayor and population to the Presbyterian Church, the only church as yet in use and used at present by all denominations, although two other edifices are being built. There H.E. was presented with an address, and gave his reply. The ladies then asked if I could not stop to speak to them about the Council and receive an address from themselves by themselves. So H.E. went for a walk round the town and its ruins with the men, one old gentleman of 80 leaning on his arm. And I received meanwhile a nice little address and a delightful box of specimen ores, and I tried to tell them all I could about the Council. I believe it will take root there, and that it may be able to do a lot of good in this rough little place where there are many difficulties to contend with. It must be a high class of missionary who can succeed here.

It took 4 hours to go up and about 3½ to come down and then there were the 28 miles by train to Robson, so it was 9 before we reached this steamer and had dinner afterwards. Mr. Barnard and his friend Mr Slade who is a shareholder and director of this new syndicate for developing the mines are on board and the latter is much pleased with what he has seen and is to report to the Board in London. They have Baron Hurch [*Hirch?*] and Rosenheim and one of the Rothschilds with them and £850,000 subscribed. Mr Barnard is managing director and has been taking up some claims just now.

After a stop in Revelstoke, recently afflicted by some quarrel between an alderman and the C.P.R., the Aberdeens went to the Guisachan Ranch for a few days on October 18.

Thursday October 17th. Sicamous

We had an awful fright last night in thinking that a telegram from Sir Mackenzie Bowell meant that we would have to return to Ottawa. However the letter to which he has referred put our fears at rest for it only meant some swearing-ins which are not required for yet awhile.

The morning mist detained us again. So we did not arrive at the Wigwam till 2 p.m. But we were very glad of this, for it was a lovely morning again and we thus saw a bit of the Columbia River which we had passed in the dark before.

We had a little ceremony of a drive and an address at Revelstoke, a poor little divided town—divided by the obstinacy of an alderman refusing to give in to the C.P.R. and so the station was taken away for half a mile and a new little town encouraged to begin and a deserted street left down below to mourn its hard fate. H.E. impressed upon the citizens of Revelstoke that by law the rule of the road in B.C. is to keep to the left contrary to the rest of Canada, which keeps to the right—this in consequence of observing a deviation from the law.

Came on here by the afternoon train and found our car of livestock here from New Westminister all ready in good trim to accompany us to Vernon to-morrow. Long talk with Mr Marpole —Mr Mara left us at Revelstoke to return to Rossland.

Their return to the Coldstream from the Guisachan was apparently hastened by the news that Sir William Van Horne, the President of the C.P.R., was coming to visit them and as there was no steamer that day they had to go by road. The journey took about six hours including a call on the Postills, a change of horses at Deer Lodge and the time it took "H.E." and the driver to fix a wheel on the wagon.

October 22nd 1895. Coldstream

It is real nice to be at home again and to settle down for another fortnight's peace. And during that time neither Marjorie not I promise to write our journals very diligently—We were very glad yesterday to accomplish at last our intention of driving from

Guisachan to this place. And indeed we had no choice when the great Sir William announced his intention of accepting our invitation for yesterday, for there was no steamer and our only plan was to leave Guisachan at 7:30 a.m. and drive right on, calling en route on Mr and Mrs Alfred Postill and the old mother, who was one of the pioneers of the district and a great character, who loves to tell of the early days when she was the only white woman and made her own candles and her own soap. Mr Postill is a great man in the district, v. keen about the Shippers Union and about getting better rates, and he is one who takes a lead in everything. We reached his place about 9, and after this the sun began to make his warmth felt and dispel the frosty feeling. It was a lovely day and Long Lake looked perfect. We changed horses at Deer Lodge and thought we should arrive in splendid time for luncheon when three miles from home one of our wheels stuck fast, and we lost well nigh half an hour and I had to run on to try to find someone to ride on to Coldstream—however by mighty continued tugging H.E. and Percy got the wheel right after the former had got a log and hoisted up the carriage as if for washing.

But we were not prepared for the vast host who awaited us, of the greater lights of the C.P.R. Not only the great Panjandrum himself, but Mr Abbott the Supt. of the division, Mr Marpole, assistant Supt., Mr Tait, general manager, Mr———Chief Engineer, Mr Clouston of the Bank of Montreal.

The supplies at the Ranch very nearly gave way, though Marjorie and I were alone conscious of the horrors of the situation and happily H.E. did not notice.

We had a delightful afternoon for our expedition to the lake site we have chosen for our future habitation. We were astonished to see the agility of Sir William over the rough places along which we took him. He was quite delighted with our site and instantly began taking notes for a sketch of the house he would design. He is quite an artist as well as a most pleasant and able man. He tells us Archie's picture by Eaton is to be a great success. He also undertakes that the C.P.R. will become customers for our fruit and vegetables which is an offer which rejoices the hearts of H.E. and Mr Kelly. Altogether the visit was quite a success....

In September 1895 Marjorie recounted at some length the wedding of Beatrice Myott, "who was staying with the Middletons" and Mr. Richard Lowe. "We picked her up looking very nice and drove to the Presbyterian church where Georgianna [who was a member of the Aberdeen's party] and Louisa Middleton, her bridesmaids, were waiting for her.... Father gave her away.... and received the guests" at the wedding breakfast. There were also shopping visits to town as "there are some very good shops here especially the stationers, dry goods, grocers, saddlers, jewellers and taxidermists." Mr. Pound, the taxidermist, "got first prize at the World's Fair.... We gave him a chipmunk and woodpecker to stuff. He has already done several birds for us." To keep Mr. Pound supplied with birds there were also calls at Megaw's and Martin's "to get some ammunition."

Various personages came to the Coldstream to see the Aberdeens and likely as not were taken "to see the fruit (as) this is a never failing means of getting rid of visitors for a bit." There were also receptions in Vernon to which the Aberdeens drove "in style" and visits to local schools including one to the Coldstream public school on the last morning of their stay in 1895. Afterwards they returned home and "at 3 Mother started in a rig" for the train ahead of time to visit the Middletons with the rest of the party following a little later. No enthusiasm was expressed over the imminent prospect of leaving the Okanagan at the end of their holiday—in October 1895.

CHAPTER VI

The Okanagan—The Last Holiday

While in Ottawa for the winter of 1895/96 the Aberdeens kept their Okanagan ranches very much in mind. In April 1896 Mr. W. C. Ricardo, their manager, came East to report on progress and to conclude the deal arranged with the C.P.R. the previous fall:

April 21st, 1896. Ottawa

Mr. Ricardo arrived from Coldstream yesterday.... (He) gives a good account of how all is going on at Coldstream and Guisachan and thinks the latter place can be made to pay its expenses with pigs. The snow was all away by the 7th or 8th of February and they have got nearly all their spring sowing done.

April 22nd, 1896

.... Mr. Ricardo returned before luncheon bringing good news to the effect that (the CPR) and he had come to satisfactory terms and we are to send fruit to four points daily at a certain definite price (for their dining cars and hotels).

Lord and Lady Aberdeen enjoyed their fifth trip to the Okanagan in October 1896. At the end of their six weeks at the Coldstream Lady Aberdeen wrote of their growing realization that as at the Guisachan irrigation was necessary for both the orchards and the hops even if the former had produced 20 tons of fruit in their first bearing year. She mentioned the very cold November that they had had with the thermometer dropping to 16° below and the consequent problem of keeping their house warm, and described the burning down of the ranch office:

December 4th 1896. Coldstream Ranch, B.C.

This is our last evening here & as are all packing up in view of our start to-morrow. I have kept my word & have sternly neglected my journal, feeling that those for whom it has been chiefly written know this place so well that a daily record of our ranching life would scarcely bring any news.

But now that we are to be on the move again, I must take a glance over these six weeks which have passed away all too quickly. When we arrived on the 16th of October the second day of the Vernon Show, it seemed as if we had such a long expanse of time before us in which to rest & go out, & sketch & ride & read, not to speak of finishing up various bits of work which we had brought with us for the purpose, & going into all the business of the ranch.

Needless to say, we now seem to have done very little of all that we intended. We have however polished off some tiresome arrears & it has been a real advantage for us to be here for a time as regards the ranch & its prospects. A. has seen much of Mr Ricardo & feels quite confident that he has found in him the right man for the place. He is very careful & economical & cuts down all possible expenses. Nevertheless there has been a good deal of extra outlay this year in fencing & in irrigation ditches, both of which were however necessities. When we came here, irrigation was not considered a necessity either for fruit or hops but our own experience & that of the settlers who have bought lots on the Estate is very clear on this point. This season has of course been peculiarly dry, but even in ordinary years we cannot possibly get on without it. This fact is proving an obstacle to the scheme of the Company which was to have formed between Messrs Stroup, hop merchants & A. for extending the hop-yards here...

The orchards have done very well for their first bearing year. Wilson the fruit expert who superintended this department, estimated that we should get 6 tons of apples from the young trees this first year & we got 20 tons. The C.P.R. has taken all our fruit large & small this year. Wilson has gone & Mr Ricardo is to find a new man. Robbins the hop man has done very well & is to go on.

Mr Ricardo's plan in taking cars of yearling cattle to Calgary to sell has answered well & we got (?) a head for two car loads. He has also shown himself very foreseeing about weaning the calves early & having the cattle down on the ranges near the house in November this year. Ordinarily no snow or real winter is expected here till Christmas—just a flurry of snow in October & then fine clear weather. We have not been fortunate in this respect. When we first arrived we had a week's real fog—the thick mist enveloping all the hills right down to the house & then a good many grey days with but little sun—& then in the second week in November down came the snow in good earnest. "Oh it will all be away in a day or two" said each person we met, but it kept on coming & the frost kept on increasing until 6° below zero was recorded at Coldstream one night & 16° below at Vernon.

Coldstream has the reputation of being a very cold house, but A. managed to increase its warmth & comfort by manufacturing movable wooden shutters which were placed every night over the innumberable doors & windows which dear old Coutts ordered to be allotted to the sitting room. There are no less than fourteen in all & the room 30 ft x 15. Stoves in which only wood is burnt warm up the room very quickly to a great heat but if you are not always on the watch they also go out before you know where you are. A. constituted himself general attendant to the stoves & it is well for him that there was no caricaturist in the party otherwise there would have been a series of pictures of His Excellency at his odd man's duties.

Before the snow came we had a good deal of riding—I have indeed ridden more than I have done for years & we all went out en famille for a couple of hours most days. We brought over a couple of horses from the North West Mounted Police from Regina, Colonel Herchmer kindly picking out two very nice ones for us & we have found them such a success that we are taking them back to Ottawa with us—they each cost $80. Archie had his dear "Wee Willie" over with him & has become quite clever about managing him & learning to open gates. Marjorie has ridden her beloved Molly, but admits that she is getting rather too heavy for her. Game has not been very plentiful this year & much to the disgust of the children, prairie chicken might not be shot at all this season. They have been so shot down that the Provincial Govt felt it necessary thus to protect them. They will soon have to take steps about the deer too. During these last few weeks our neighbours have been going out blazing away & massacring dozens of the poor creatures who are quite unfit for food & whom they do not even bring down.

The regular hunting parties who have gone out for a month or two camping in the mountains after big game have also had but poor sport. Our neighbours Mr & Mrs Jones-Williams & the two Miss Gordons, who have taken Will's place, were out for over a month with a large party, twenty pack-ponies & Indians & all the rest of it but got very little & did not have the chance of a bear at all. However the chicks have at least had the chance of *seeing* some fine stags nearer than they have ever done before & as for Archie, he has been very happy shooting squirrels & magpies in the intervals of his Latin & French & arithmetic which have been gone on with steadily all the time we have been here.

Now as to outstanding events. First of course amongst these, comes the burning down of the poor office which was built with so much care last year. It was a nice little place & answered its purpose perfectly. There had been deposited the precious cypher box containing the only means of private communication with the Home authorities as well as others for communicating with the Ministers here & Washington & so on. There was also all current official correspondence & a great many private papers & letters belonging both to H.E. and Captain Sinclair. The latter also had his two rifles, his gun & a lot ammunition there. This room boasted of the one open fireplace in the place. It was a brick one & carefully fenced round with a high nursery fender. It was not sufficient however for warmth & only the day before the fire H.E. had introduced a new pet stove of his own but it had not yet been put in use.

On Sunday Nov. 1st Capt. S. had been sitting in the office all the afternoon. The fire was nearly out at seven, but was then raked out & the lamp removed. We had our usual evening service with all the men & then dined. Between twelve & one H.E. & I being the only members of the house still up, we heard a couple of pops. "It's a skunk" says H.E. & runs for his rifle. A further succession of pops makes me run out after him & he then said "Can anyone be letting off fireworks?" & then it flashed on us what it really meant & that there was all that gunpowder in the office. We rang the alarm bell to the ranch, & I ran up to waken the men upstairs & Capt. Sinclair & get the children dressed in case of the ranch-house catching fire from sparks. H.E. meanwhile ran across to the office which still looked quite dark from our side but which was enveloped in a mass of smoke. When he looked in at the window, all one side of the room was in flames. He was quickly joined by everyone from the ranch & I suppose something could have been done had we had water near enough or enough men for a line down to the stream. But on Captain Sinclair throwing a log in at the window in order to make an opening to get at the cypher box, the flames burst out in fury & explosion followed explosion, making it quite clear that it would be folly for anyone to venture inside. So we just had to stand by & look on & devote our energies to protecting our house & the other ranch buildings. Happily the wind *just* took the sparks past our house & there had been a great deal of rain so that by Mr Browell keeping a constant pour of water over the verandah & dislodging the sparks as they alighted no harm was done. One of the bullets was found on the verandah & a great piece of burning shingle alighted on the barn roof down below. It was fortunate that no *public* official document was burnt which could not be replaced. Nevertheless there was some Tupper private correspondence which it is a nuisance to have lost & Capt. S. lost a variety of small personal treasures & possessions which cannot be replaced. The building itself was insured for $400.

Lady Aberdeen went on to comment on the Agriculture Show in Vernon that year, her work with the Women's Council in Vernon (she was responsible for setting up the National Council of Women in Canada), a concert held on behalf of the "reading room" which was initiated by the Aberdeens to keep the "young bachelors" out of the saloons, a costume ball which they gave in the still unused jam factory and her concern during a visit to the Guisachan for an impoverished couple unlikely to succeed as pioneers.

December 4th, 1896 (cont.)

As regards public events in Vernon there are several to chronicle. First the Show the day we arrived which was a much better affair then that of last year. The Women's Council had the charge of all the industrial part and of the bread and butter and made quite a success of it. The same evening Mr. Outerbridge badgered H.E. into staying for a Church of England concert and appeared himself in his well known lavender gloves sewn with black in his role of chairman and singer. Then I had an Executive of the Women's Council at which everybody seemed rather depressed—this was followed by the Annual Meeting which marked the turning of the corner and now they are all in very good heart, preparing for cooking classes in February under Miss Livingstone's management and they are also making preparations for opening a Cottage Hospital. It was their failure to get a Hospital started last year which disheartened them, but they were somewhat ambitious in their ideas and the local doctors being all at daggers drawn and refusing to meet one another made it difficult. This summer the visitation of typhoid fever and the deaths which were the result of want of nursing brought the real need of a hospital of some sort home. The Provincial Government are inclined to give a grant in assistance of the project. I think we may claim that the experiment of starting a Council in this small place has been successful. Like all little towns it is full of bickering and gossip and little cliques in opposition to one another. The Council has been the means of the leading ladies of the different churches meeting one another and working together at something and also has led them to take an interest in matters going on in other parts of the country. They all agree on this and Mrs. Cochrane, the President, who has been re-elected has done very well. Miss Coghlan, the school teacher is now Secretary.

The next excitement was a Concert on behalf of the Reading Room—an institution which has become quite popular. Two years ago when it was started there were great doubts about it being able to exist and the first year they only kept it open during the winter. Last year, however, they found a young fellow called (name omitted in original) well educated but delicate to take charge of it for $15 a month. He took an immense interest in it and made it go and begged to keep it open during the summer with the result that about as many came as during the winter and a little circulatory library was started. Before this reading room was opened the many young bachelors about had no place of (?) save the saloons. The concert was quite a success. Miss Warren, a semi-professional singer, daughter of Col. Warren, who had come out lately from England and settled his sons at Grand Prairie, was brought in to sing. Mr. Henderson, Miss Vidler and (?) played banjoes and mandolines—Marjorie and Archie doing the same—and H.E. giving a little lecture on the House of Lords. It was a bitterly cold night, but there was a capital attendance and a profit of 75 dollars. This was on the 12th and on the 19th we gathered in the jam factory the most brilliant assembly etc. etc. that had ever been seen in the inland of B.C. But for the details of this see the Vernon News. We thought that we ought to do something neighbourly of this kind and it seemed to go off very well. Mrs. Henderson and Miss Vidler appeared as an engaged couple and Mr. Henderson and Mr. Hankey, the two bankers, as reconciled friends. They also had not "spoken" to one another for some time. The children came in for a bit but slept in the car. Mr. Ricardo managed all the decorating, etc. very well and the jam factory was much admired. We wish however that it could have been put to its proper use.

Then we went down to Guisachan for a night, inspecting everything there and seeing a good many of the people and A quite pleased at the way the plan of making the place practically (?) a hog farm is turning out. Saw Beatrice's (Lowe) baby who is quite a credit to her and arranged with Louisa Tremaine to go to Mrs. Thomson at Armstrong. Also saw poor little Mrs. Dundas—a young bride from Scotland who married one of the Dundases of

Arneston who came out here. It was pathetic to see her looking very much a bride in her little two roomed shack with her pretty wedding presents about and her Japanese rugs, the gift of Mr. Jamieson and guessing what the future would probably be, neither of the pair having a cent he having been somewhat wild and having broken most of his bones and his 20 acres not giving much prospects of providing sustenance. It is cruel to let these sort of people come out here—it is bad enough for the men but for the women it is terrible especially when the children come and there is no help to be got.

For ten days the CPR was blocked with heavy snow falls and slides and no trains could get through to the Coast... I began to think that I should scarcely get through to Vancouver and Victoria for my Women's Council meetings. However, I just managed it (but) it was a grind... We are rather disappointed that the snow and severe weather makes it seem unadvisable for us to pay our projected visit to Rossland (which they later visited in 1898), but it would not do to be blocked there. Everyone is full of the place and it is growing by leaps and bounds. Last year it had a population of 2,000—now it has 6,000—and they talk of 15,000 next year. There are many who fear that there may be a comedown. All the country is full of mines if only there were the capital to work them. Here quite near Vernon is the Morning Glory mine but it is in the hands of men without money and they sell 10 cent shares in order to live on the proceeds. Governor Dewdney is very certain as to the future of all this country from a mining point of view.

Now I must stop. Otherwise this brief account of our stay here will become no longer brief, but there are many things I should have liked to have added. I have said nothing about out expedition to the meadows to visit old Mr. Hardie and daughter, Mr. and Mrs. Haldane's prodigies, nor about the children's skating pond, nor about our visit to the settlers, nor about church affairs in Vernon nor about Mr. Erskine Knowles the missionary sent for Coldstream and Lumby but who has not proved quite the man. He has left now.

Lord Aberdeen's term was not scheduled to end until 1899 but, as he pointed out in *We Twa*,[1] "the expenses of our régime had been very heavy. Our plan of residing at the different centres, in addition to Ottawa, and entertaining at each... had added largely to our burdens... Coldstream's failure to be a source of income not to speak of the outlays required there, had placed us at a disadvantage."

At the end of July 1898, four months before they returned to Britain in November, the Aberdeens paid a brief visit to the Okanagan. As they were returning East, Lady Aberdeen spoke of her inspection of the new hospital (see above) in Vernon, the excellent prospects for the hop and fruit crop and the importance of packing the apples properly, a picnic that they had at the head of Long Lake, the progress of various settlers and finally, the farewell given to them as they boarded the train:

En route between St. Paul and Sault Ste. Marie. August 6th, 1898

. . . And now why try to harrow(?) my feelings by writing of out last three days there for Thursday the 28th was spent at Vernon meeting the Women's Council, seeing their hospital, meeting their Hospital directors who jumped at the idea of a Victorian Nurse (Lady Aberdeen was responsible for establishing the Victorian Order of Nurses) when they found the expense so moderate and even talked to two, calling on Mr. Cameron who was ill and Mrs. Cochrane and finally attending a dance given in the new Bank Building by the Lawn Tennis Club and over which Mr. & Mrs. Henderson and Capt. & Mrs. Sutherland presided. Mr. Browell was there and acted as ADC again although fully installed as manager of the BX ranch. It had been baking all day up in the nineties and very near 100° inside the car and it was refreshing to drive out at night and to find a cloak not superfluous. Just Gunn, Georgie, Turner and ourselves were in possession of the house as Mr. Ricardo and Mr. Hodges had moved into the old house last week. Their Chinaman did nicely for us with our old friend Sam from the Ranch to help. Indeed the cooking was quite an improvement on Haswell whose performances during this trip have been the reverse of successful! Through the day the heat was very great and the sun scorching, but in the evening and morning there was a pleasant breeze and the nights were quite cool. The whole place has taken a great step forward since we saw it eighteen months (ago) and the development of the orchards strikes one most of all . . . Mr. Raeburn, the new foreman . . . has proved a great success . . . both in his general management, in his knowledge of all the secrets of pruning etc. and above all in his experience of packing which is considered by Mr. Ricardo as three-fifths of the battle. The orchards now look beautifully cared for the trees have grown marvellously, so that they look quite established and old instead of young plantations about which there is only hope to feed on. The Northern Spy trees are bearing this year and many of the trees were simply laden with fruit. Mr. Ricardo estimated having 15 tons of apples to dispose of—but he has 50 and it is all sold to two wholesale firms—at 2½¢ a lb.—they will be picking and packing in three weeks.

The new fruit packing house is also very business like and the little wooden boxes are now being made at the rate of 100 boxes a day by a boy by means of a simple machine—the same way with the apple boxes and crates—the wood is supplied in stacks of the right size and it is made up by our own men. There will also be a great crop of plums and a good one of pears—we are to begin to make vinegar with the rejected apples this autumn and the growing of vegetables will go forward on a large scale now that a wholesale vegetable merchant in the Kootenay undertakes to purchase them. For packing purposes the fruit is all sorted out into different sizes, which is a great secret(?) here... and then all have to be pressed(?) down and for this Raeburn has himself invented a machine.

All round the house is nothing but white clover now and near the fence where the irrigation ditch used to run is a vegetable garden... It is rather sad that the growth of the orchards is quite shutting out the nice vista up the valley terminating in the familiar blue Camel's Hump.

The hop yards are also looking very flourishing including the new ones opposite the Ranch buildings.... We now work six kilns at the cost of 17 where we used to work three at 13 (sic)... Ricardo expects to clear double what he estimated unless any unforeseen disaster occurs. He and Robins look upon the hops as the most certain crop we have and will not allow that there is any speculation about it—at least less than there is in any other crop dependent on weather. There has been so much rain this year that we have not had to use irrigation at all nor the plot holders either. Mr. Ricardo and Mr. Hodges dined with us and afterwards we inspected the books, the labour roll and all sorts of other documents which appear to be beautifully kept. Mr. Hodges (the bookkeeper) is a valuable man... and a great comfort to Mr. Ricardo. Nevertheless, Mr. Browell is keenly missed, for he was as a son in the house, full of brightness and gentleness. But of course it was a great promotion for him to get the managership of the BX Ranch at the age of 22. He gets $60.00 a month—but he must feel pretty lonely... Miss Ricardo (has) arrived at Vernon (to) be with her brother for the winter...

On the Saturday we had a regular party . . . for luncheon. Then we all proceeded to the other side to the place the children call the 'race course' for a round-up of the cattle . . . (and) then a picnic at the head of the Long Lake which was quite a success . . . The clear lake looked lovely and we fortunately came upon Mr. Moss (?) who had been painting there all day . . . We left the party to go on the Lake for a row whilst we went to pay farewell calls to the plot holders including Mr. and Mrs. Twidle who have now got three lots and are doing fine—sensible looking people with two young nieces. The Denisons too are getting on nicely though he was very ill this spring. Turner, Streatfield, the Websters and the Venables are all still there prospering more or less. The Websters were burnt out and are re-building. Stewart has a jolly little house with a lovely garden in the dip under the great stone . . . We had a hurried dinner with the Markleys, Mr. Acland and Mr. Brown . . . and then drove in for farewell festivities at Vernon—special platform erected outside—Chinese lanterns, decoration—address from the Mayor and citizens—fireworks and farewell reception with a further rather drawn out farewell at the station for the engine of our special train could not find the heart to go and groaned and fumed in the attempt considerably. Morrison and Mrs. Morrison had come up from Guisachan to see us and A sent for their children to see the fireworks. All going well there and it is to pay its way this year, they say, without doubt. Old Mrs. Hardie and her daughter came down in a rig . . . Mr. Thomson and Louisa Tremaine met us at Vernon and came on with us to Armstrong on our special and we went to see the house although it was midnight.

I must not (write) more about Coldstream or I shall never come to the end, but I must record that the Hospital Director and Local Council Executive (decided on) one if not two Victorian Nurses and the Council heartily decided to help in the matter of a paid Secretary . . .

The Aberdeens saw the Coldstream for the last time seventeen years later while on a visit to Canada and the United States in the winter of 1915-16. Lady Aberdeen recalled the marvellous memories which it conjured up. They had been delighted to go there during the first fall of their term as Governor-General. They had entered enthusiastically and expensively into the plan for the great irrigation network not only for their own property but for the smaller lots that they had sold. They became expert about the various varieties of apples and which would grow best in the Okanagan. The small fruits could always be sold near home and the C.P.R. promised a market through its railways and a new chain of hotels. High freight rates were, then as now, against them, but even so the future looked promising. The arrival of new settlers and the purchase of land by men of means like Lord Shaughnessy and Lord Grey reflected confidence in the future of the Vernon district. The only problem was that of surviving the development of the ranch including its irrigation system. The best of business advisers promised them success. "But the years came and went and the golden age predicted always receded and always more capital was called for so as not to lose what had already been invested.... Neither the purchase money nor all that was spent on development ever came back and the results of our investment in B.C. have been very sad."[1] Lord Woolavington joined them as a partner and eventually took over the property entirely in 1921.

Lady Aberdeen thought that a friend who had written to her recently from the Okanagan had summed up the circumstances rather well in saying: "It is hard for poor persons to stay and keep their orchards up to the mark. But it is truly wonderful how optimistic everybody is. It must mean a brighter future. People of B.C. are certainly not despondent. I think the climate is so invigorating that is impossible to be other than cheerful, and the longer one lives in the country the better one likes it, in spite of every drawback from a financial standpoint. Other than those, there are no drawbacks."[2]

Notes

CHAPTER VI

[1] *We Twa*, p. 90.
[2] *We Twa*, p. 91.

INDEX